Running Log Book
by

_____

_____

_____

Year: _____ Month: _____ Week: _____ Weekly Goal: _____

Monday	Date:		Burns Target: 2
Notes:	Route:	Indian Springs loop	
	Distance: 5 miles	Time:	
	Weight: over	Speed:	
	Burn Cals: 950 ?	Heart Rate: 195	
	Weather: Nice	Breathing: heavy	
	How I Felt: Like Crap		
	Injuries: cut my finger		
	Overall Thoughts: Busted 3 x's. Was at night so kinda scary..		

Tuesday	Date:		Burns Target:
Notes:	Route:		
	Distance:	Time:	
	Weight:	Speed:	
	Burn Cals:	Heart Rate:	
	Weather:	Breathing:	
	How I Felt:		
	Injuries:		
	Overall Thoughts:		

Wednesday	Date:		Burns Target:
Notes:	Route:		
	Distance:	Time:	
	Weight:	Speed:	
	Burn Cals:	Heart Rate:	
	Weather:	Breathing:	
	How I Felt:		
	Injuries:		
	Overall Thoughts:		

Thursday	Date:		Burns Target:
Notes:	Route:		
	Distance:	Time:	
	Weight:	Speed:	
	Burn Cals:	Heart Rate:	
	Weather:	Breathing:	
	How I Felt:		
	Injuries:		
	Overall Thoughts:		

Friday	Date:		Burns Target:	
Notes: First year Meet	Route:			
	Distance:	2 miles	Time:	
	Weight:		Speed:	
	Burn Cals:		Heart Rate:	
	Weather:		Breathing:	
	How I Felt:	OK		
	Injuries:	None		
	Overall Thoughts:	Hard but fun		

Saturday	Date:		Burns Target:	
Notes:	Route:			
	Distance:		Time:	
	Weight:		Speed:	
	Burn Cals:		Heart Rate:	
	Weather:		Breathing:	
	How I Felt:			
	Injuries:			
	Overall Thoughts:			

Sunday	Date:		Burns Target:	
Notes:	Route:			
	Distance:		Time:	
	Weight:		Speed:	
	Burn Cals:		Heart Rate:	
	Weather:		Breathing:	
	How I Felt:			
	Injuries:			
	Overall Thoughts:			

Weekly Review

Total Distance:		Weight loss:	
Average Speed:		Total Hours:	
Average Heart Rate:		Total Burns:	

Notes / Thoughts:

Year: .... Month: .... Week: .... Weekly Goal: ....

Monday	Date:	Burns Target:
Notes:	Route:	
	Distance:	Time:
	Weight:	Speed:
	Burn Cals:	Heart Rate:
	Weather:	Breathing:
	How I Felt:	
	Injuries:	
	Overall Thoughts:	

Tuesday	Date:	Burns Target:
Notes:	Route:	
	Distance:	Time:
	Weight:	Speed:
	Burn Cals:	Heart Rate:
	Weather:	Breathing:
	How I Felt:	
	Injuries:	
	Overall Thoughts:	

Wednesday	Date:	Burns Target:
Notes:	Route:	
	Distance:	Time:
	Weight:	Speed:
	Burn Cals:	Heart Rate:
	Weather:	Breathing:
	How I Felt:	
	Injuries:	
	Overall Thoughts:	

Thursday	Date:	Burns Target:
Notes:	Route:	
	Distance:	Time:
	Weight:	Speed:
	Burn Cals:	Heart Rate:
	Weather:	Breathing:
	How I Felt:	
	Injuries:	
	Overall Thoughts:	

Friday	Date:		Burns Target:	
Notes:	Route:			
	Distance:		Time:	
	Weight:		Speed:	
	Burn Cals:		Heart Rate:	
	Weather:		Breathing:	
	How I Felt:			
	Injuries:			
	Overall Thoughts:			

Saturday	Date:		Burns Target:	
Notes:	Route:			
	Distance:		Time:	
	Weight:		Speed:	
	Burn Cals:		Heart Rate:	
	Weather:		Breathing:	
	How I Felt:			
	Injuries:			
	Overall Thoughts:			

Sunday	Date:		Burns Target:	
Notes:	Route:			
	Distance:		Time:	
	Weight:		Speed:	
	Burn Cals:		Heart Rate:	
	Weather:		Breathing:	
	How I Felt:			
	Injuries:			
	Overall Thoughts:			

Weekly Review

Total Distance:		Weight loss:	
Average Speed:		Total Hours:	
Average Heart Rate:		Total Burns:	

Notes / Thoughts:

Year: _____ Month: _____ Week: _____ Weekly Goal: _____

Monday	Date:		Burns Target:
Notes:	Route:		
	Distance:	Time:	
	Weight:	Speed:	
	Burn Cals:	Heart Rate:	
	Weather:	Breathing:	
	How I Felt:		
	Injuries:		
	Overall Thoughts:		

Tuesday	Date:		Burns Target:
Notes:	Route:		
	Distance:	Time:	
	Weight:	Speed:	
	Burn Cals:	Heart Rate:	
	Weather:	Breathing:	
	How I Felt:		
	Injuries:		
	Overall Thoughts:		

Wednesday	Date:		Burns Target:
Notes:	Route:		
	Distance:	Time:	
	Weight:	Speed:	
	Burn Cals:	Heart Rate:	
	Weather:	Breathing:	
	How I Felt:		
	Injuries:		
	Overall Thoughts:		

Thursday	Date:		Burns Target:
Notes:	Route:		
	Distance:	Time:	
	Weight:	Speed:	
	Burn Cals:	Heart Rate:	
	Weather:	Breathing:	
	How I Felt:		
	Injuries:		
	Overall Thoughts:		

Friday	Date:		Burns Target:
Notes:	Route:		
	Distance:		Time:
	Weight:		Speed:
	Burn Cals:		Heart Rate:
	Weather:		Breathing:
	How I Felt:		
	Injuries:		
	Overall Thoughts:		

Saturday	Date:		Burns Target:
Notes:	Route:		
	Distance:		Time:
	Weight:		Speed:
	Burn Cals:		Heart Rate:
	Weather:		Breathing:
	How I Felt:		
	Injuries:		
	Overall Thoughts:		

Sunday	Date:		Burns Target:
Notes:	Route:		
	Distance:		Time:
	Weight:		Speed:
	Burn Cals:		Heart Rate:
	Weather:		Breathing:
	How I Felt:		
	Injuries:		
	Overall Thoughts:		

Weekly Review			
Total Distance:		Weight loss:	
Average Speed:		Total Hours:	
Average Heart Rate:		Total Burns:	
Notes / Thoughts:			

Year: .... Month: .... Week: .... Weekly Goal: ....

Monday	Date:	Burns Target:

Notes:

Route:	
Distance:	Time:
Weight:	Speed:
Burn Cals:	Heart Rate:
Weather:	Breathing:
How I Felt:	
Injuries:	
Overall Thoughts:	

Tuesday	Date:	Burns Target:

Notes:

Route:	
Distance:	Time:
Weight:	Speed:
Burn Cals:	Heart Rate:
Weather:	Breathing:
How I Felt:	
Injuries:	
Overall Thoughts:	

Wednesday	Date:	Burns Target:

Notes:

Route:	
Distance:	Time:
Weight:	Speed:
Burn Cals:	Heart Rate:
Weather:	Breathing:
How I Felt:	
Injuries:	
Overall Thoughts:	

Thursday	Date:	Burns Target:

Notes:

Route:	
Distance:	Time:
Weight:	Speed:
Burn Cals:	Heart Rate:
Weather:	Breathing:
How I Felt:	
Injuries:	
Overall Thoughts:	

Friday	Date:		Burns Target:	
Notes:	Route:			
	Distance:		Time:	
	Weight:		Speed:	
	Burn Cals:		Heart Rate:	
	Weather:		Breathing:	
	How I Felt:			
	Injuries:			
	Overall Thoughts:			

Saturday	Date:		Burns Target:	
Notes:	Route:			
	Distance:		Time:	
	Weight:		Speed:	
	Burn Cals:		Heart Rate:	
	Weather:		Breathing:	
	How I Felt:			
	Injuries:			
	Overall Thoughts:			

Sunday	Date:		Burns Target:	
Notes:	Route:			
	Distance:		Time:	
	Weight:		Speed:	
	Burn Cals:		Heart Rate:	
	Weather:		Breathing:	
	How I Felt:			
	Injuries:			
	Overall Thoughts:			

Weekly Review

Total Distance:		Weight loss:	
Average Speed:		Total Hours:	
Average Heart Rate:		Total Burns:	

Notes / Thoughts:

Year: .... Month: .... Week: .... Weekly Goal: ....

Monday	Date:	Burns Target:
Notes:	Route:	
	Distance:	Time:
	Weight:	Speed:
	Burn Cals:	Heart Rate:
	Weather:	Breathing:
	How I Felt:	
	Injuries:	
	Overall Thoughts:	

Tuesday	Date:	Burns Target:
Notes:	Route:	
	Distance:	Time:
	Weight:	Speed:
	Burn Cals:	Heart Rate:
	Weather:	Breathing:
	How I Felt:	
	Injuries:	
	Overall Thoughts:	

Wednesday	Date:	Burns Target:
Notes:	Route:	
	Distance:	Time:
	Weight:	Speed:
	Burn Cals:	Heart Rate:
	Weather:	Breathing:
	How I Felt:	
	Injuries:	
	Overall Thoughts:	

Thursday	Date:	Burns Target:
Notes:	Route:	
	Distance:	Time:
	Weight:	Speed:
	Burn Cals:	Heart Rate:
	Weather:	Breathing:
	How I Felt:	
	Injuries:	
	Overall Thoughts:	

Friday	Date:		Burns Target:	
Notes:	Route:			
	Distance:		Time:	
	Weight:		Speed:	
	Burn Cals:		Heart Rate:	
	Weather:		Breathing:	
	How I Felt:			
	Injuries:			
	Overall Thoughts:			

Saturday	Date:		Burns Target:	
Notes:	Route:			
	Distance:		Time:	
	Weight:		Speed:	
	Burn Cals:		Heart Rate:	
	Weather:		Breathing:	
	How I Felt:			
	Injuries:			
	Overall Thoughts:			

Sunday	Date:		Burns Target:	
Notes:	Route:			
	Distance:		Time:	
	Weight:		Speed:	
	Burn Cals:		Heart Rate:	
	Weather:		Breathing:	
	How I Felt:			
	Injuries:			
	Overall Thoughts:			

Weekly Review			
Total Distance:		Weight loss:	
Average Speed:		Total Hours:	
Average Heart Rate:		Total Burns:	
Notes / Thoughts:			

Year:.............. Month:.............. Week:.............. Weekly Goal:..........

Monday	Date:	Burns Target:
Notes:	Route:	
	Distance:	Time:
	Weight:	Speed:
	Burn Cals:	Heart Rate:
	Weather:	Breathing:
	How I Felt:	
	Injuries:	
	Overall Thoughts:	

Tuesday	Date:	Burns Target:
Notes:	Route:	
	Distance:	Time:
	Weight:	Speed:
	Burn Cals:	Heart Rate:
	Weather:	Breathing:
	How I Felt:	
	Injuries:	
	Overall Thoughts:	

Wednesday	Date:	Burns Target:
Notes:	Route:	
	Distance:	Time:
	Weight:	Speed:
	Burn Cals:	Heart Rate:
	Weather:	Breathing:
	How I Felt:	
	Injuries:	
	Overall Thoughts:	

Thursday	Date:	Burns Target:
Notes:	Route:	
	Distance:	Time:
	Weight:	Speed:
	Burn Cals:	Heart Rate:
	Weather:	Breathing:
	How I Felt:	
	Injuries:	
	Overall Thoughts:	

Friday	Date:		Burns Target:
Notes:	Route:		
	Distance:		Time:
	Weight:		Speed:
	Burn Cals:		Heart Rate:
	Weather:		Breathing:
	How I Felt:		
	Injuries:		
	Overall Thoughts:		

Saturday	Date:		Burns Target:
Notes:	Route:		
	Distance:		Time:
	Weight:		Speed:
	Burn Cals:		Heart Rate:
	Weather:		Breathing:
	How I Felt:		
	Injuries:		
	Overall Thoughts:		

Sunday	Date:		Burns Target:
Notes:	Route:		
	Distance:		Time:
	Weight:		Speed:
	Burn Cals:		Heart Rate:
	Weather:		Breathing:
	How I Felt:		
	Injuries:		
	Overall Thoughts:		

Weekly Review

Total Distance:		Weight loss:	
Average Speed:		Total Hours:	
Average Heart Rate:		Total Burns:	

Notes / Thoughts:

Year:_____ Month:_____ Week:_____ Weekly Goal:_____

Monday	Date:		Burns Target:
Notes:	Route:		
	Distance:	Time:	
	Weight:	Speed:	
	Burn Cals:	Heart Rate:	
	Weather:	Breathing:	
	How I Felt:		
	Injuries:		
	Overall Thoughts:		

Tuesday	Date:		Burns Target:
Notes:	Route:		
	Distance:	Time:	
	Weight:	Speed:	
	Burn Cals:	Heart Rate:	
	Weather:	Breathing:	
	How I Felt:		
	Injuries:		
	Overall Thoughts:		

Wednesday	Date:		Burns Target:
Notes:	Route:		
	Distance:	Time:	
	Weight:	Speed:	
	Burn Cals:	Heart Rate:	
	Weather:	Breathing:	
	How I Felt:		
	Injuries:		
	Overall Thoughts:		

Thursday	Date:		Burns Target:
Notes:	Route:		
	Distance:	Time:	
	Weight:	Speed:	
	Burn Cals:	Heart Rate:	
	Weather:	Breathing:	
	How I Felt:		
	Injuries:		
	Overall Thoughts:		

Friday	Date:		Burns Target:	
Notes:	Route:			
	Distance:		Time:	
	Weight:		Speed:	
	Burn Cals:		Heart Rate:	
	Weather:		Breathing:	
	How I Felt:			
	Injuries:			
	Overall Thoughts:			

Saturday	Date:		Burns Target:	
Notes:	Route:			
	Distance:		Time:	
	Weight:		Speed:	
	Burn Cals:		Heart Rate:	
	Weather:		Breathing:	
	How I Felt:			
	Injuries:			
	Overall Thoughts:			

Sunday	Date:		Burns Target:	
Notes:	Route:			
	Distance:		Time:	
	Weight:		Speed:	
	Burn Cals:		Heart Rate:	
	Weather:		Breathing:	
	How I Felt:			
	Injuries:			
	Overall Thoughts:			

Weekly Review

Total Distance:		Weight loss:	
Average Speed:		Total Hours:	
Average Heart Rate:		Total Burns:	

Notes / Thoughts:

Year: .... Month: .... Week: .... Weekly Goal: ....

Monday	Date:		Burns Target:
Notes:	Route:		
	Distance:	Time:	
	Weight:	Speed:	
	Burn Cals:	Heart Rate:	
	Weather:	Breathing:	
	How I Felt:		
	Injuries:		
	Overall Thoughts:		

Tuesday	Date:		Burns Target:
Notes:	Route:		
	Distance:	Time:	
	Weight:	Speed:	
	Burn Cals:	Heart Rate:	
	Weather:	Breathing:	
	How I Felt:		
	Injuries:		
	Overall Thoughts:		

Wednesday	Date:		Burns Target:
Notes:	Route:		
	Distance:	Time:	
	Weight:	Speed:	
	Burn Cals:	Heart Rate:	
	Weather:	Breathing:	
	How I Felt:		
	Injuries:		
	Overall Thoughts:		

Thursday	Date:		Burns Target:
Notes:	Route:		
	Distance:	Time:	
	Weight:	Speed:	
	Burn Cals:	Heart Rate:	
	Weather:	Breathing:	
	How I Felt:		
	Injuries:		
	Overall Thoughts:		

Friday	Date:		Burns Target:
Notes:	Route:		
	Distance:	Time:	
	Weight:	Speed:	
	Burn Cals:	Heart Rate:	
	Weather:	Breathing:	
	How I Felt:		
	Injuries:		
	Overall Thoughts:		

Saturday	Date:		Burns Target:
Notes:	Route:		
	Distance:	Time:	
	Weight:	Speed:	
	Burn Cals:	Heart Rate:	
	Weather:	Breathing:	
	How I Felt:		
	Injuries:		
	Overall Thoughts:		

Sunday	Date:		Burns Target:
Notes:	Route:		
	Distance:	Time:	
	Weight:	Speed:	
	Burn Cals:	Heart Rate:	
	Weather:	Breathing:	
	How I Felt:		
	Injuries:		
	Overall Thoughts:		

Weekly Review

Total Distance:		Weight loss:	
Average Speed:		Total Hours:	
Average Heart Rate:		Total Burns:	

Notes / Thoughts:

Year: _____ Month: _____ Week: _____ Weekly Goal: _____

Monday	Date:	Burns Target:	
Notes:	Route:		
	Distance:	Time:	
	Weight:	Speed:	
	Burn Cals:	Heart Rate:	
	Weather:	Breathing:	
	How I Felt:		
	Injuries:		
	Overall Thoughts:		

Tuesday	Date:	Burns Target:	
Notes:	Route:		
	Distance:	Time:	
	Weight:	Speed:	
	Burn Cals:	Heart Rate:	
	Weather:	Breathing:	
	How I Felt:		
	Injuries:		
	Overall Thoughts:		

Wednesday	Date:	Burns Target:	
Notes:	Route:		
	Distance:	Time:	
	Weight:	Speed:	
	Burn Cals:	Heart Rate:	
	Weather:	Breathing:	
	How I Felt:		
	Injuries:		
	Overall Thoughts:		

Thursday	Date:	Burns Target:	
Notes:	Route:		
	Distance:	Time:	
	Weight:	Speed:	
	Burn Cals:	Heart Rate:	
	Weather:	Breathing:	
	How I Felt:		
	Injuries:		
	Overall Thoughts:		

Friday	Date:		Burns Target:	
Notes:	Route:			
	Distance:		Time:	
	Weight:		Speed:	
	Burn Cals:		Heart Rate:	
	Weather:		Breathing:	
	How I Felt:			
	Injuries:			
	Overall Thoughts:			

Saturday	Date:		Burns Target:	
Notes:	Route:			
	Distance:		Time:	
	Weight:		Speed:	
	Burn Cals:		Heart Rate:	
	Weather:		Breathing:	
	How I Felt:			
	Injuries:			
	Overall Thoughts:			

Sunday	Date:		Burns Target:	
Notes:	Route:			
	Distance:		Time:	
	Weight:		Speed:	
	Burn Cals:		Heart Rate:	
	Weather:		Breathing:	
	How I Felt:			
	Injuries:			
	Overall Thoughts:			

Weekly Review			
Total Distance:		Weight loss:	
Average Speed:		Total Hours:	
Average Heart Rate:		Total Burns:	
Notes / Thoughts:			

Year: .... Month: .... Week: .... Weekly Goal: ....

Monday	Date:		Burns Target:	
Notes:	Route:			
	Distance:		Time:	
	Weight:		Speed:	
	Burn Cals:		Heart Rate:	
	Weather:		Breathing:	
	How I Felt:			
	Injuries:			
	Overall Thoughts:			

Tuesday	Date:		Burns Target:	
Notes:	Route:			
	Distance:		Time:	
	Weight:		Speed:	
	Burn Cals:		Heart Rate:	
	Weather:		Breathing:	
	How I Felt:			
	Injuries:			
	Overall Thoughts:			

Wednesday	Date:		Burns Target:	
Notes:	Route:			
	Distance:		Time:	
	Weight:		Speed:	
	Burn Cals:		Heart Rate:	
	Weather:		Breathing:	
	How I Felt:			
	Injuries:			
	Overall Thoughts:			

Thursday	Date:		Burns Target:	
Notes:	Route:			
	Distance:		Time:	
	Weight:		Speed:	
	Burn Cals:		Heart Rate:	
	Weather:		Breathing:	
	How I Felt:			
	Injuries:			
	Overall Thoughts:			

Friday	Date:		Burns Target:
Notes:	Route:		
	Distance:		Time:
	Weight:		Speed:
	Burn Cals:		Heart Rate:
	Weather:		Breathing:
	How I Felt:		
	Injuries:		
	Overall Thoughts:		

Saturday	Date:		Burns Target:
Notes:	Route:		
	Distance:		Time:
	Weight:		Speed:
	Burn Cals:		Heart Rate:
	Weather:		Breathing:
	How I Felt:		
	Injuries:		
	Overall Thoughts:		

Sunday	Date:		Burns Target:
Notes:	Route:		
	Distance:		Time:
	Weight:		Speed:
	Burn Cals:		Heart Rate:
	Weather:		Breathing:
	How I Felt:		
	Injuries:		
	Overall Thoughts:		

Weekly Review			
Total Distance:		Weight loss:	
Average Speed:		Total Hours:	
Average Heart Rate:		Total Burns:	
Notes / Thoughts:			

Year: _____ Month: _____ Week: _____ Weekly Goal: _____

Monday	Date:	Burns Target:
Notes:	Route:	
	Distance:	Time:
	Weight:	Speed:
	Burn Cals:	Heart Rate:
	Weather:	Breathing:
	How I Felt:	
	Injuries:	
	Overall Thoughts:	

Tuesday	Date:	Burns Target:
Notes:	Route:	
	Distance:	Time:
	Weight:	Speed:
	Burn Cals:	Heart Rate:
	Weather:	Breathing:
	How I Felt:	
	Injuries:	
	Overall Thoughts:	

Wednesday	Date:	Burns Target:
Notes:	Route:	
	Distance:	Time:
	Weight:	Speed:
	Burn Cals:	Heart Rate:
	Weather:	Breathing:
	How I Felt:	
	Injuries:	
	Overall Thoughts:	

Thursday	Date:	Burns Target:
Notes:	Route:	
	Distance:	Time:
	Weight:	Speed:
	Burn Cals:	Heart Rate:
	Weather:	Breathing:
	How I Felt:	
	Injuries:	
	Overall Thoughts:	

Friday	Date:		Burns Target:	
Notes:	Route:			
	Distance:		Time:	
	Weight:		Speed:	
	Burn Cals:		Heart Rate:	
	Weather:		Breathing:	
	How I Felt:			
	Injuries:			
	Overall Thoughts:			

Saturday	Date:		Burns Target:	
Notes:	Route:			
	Distance:		Time:	
	Weight:		Speed:	
	Burn Cals:		Heart Rate:	
	Weather:		Breathing:	
	How I Felt:			
	Injuries:			
	Overall Thoughts:			

Sunday	Date:		Burns Target:	
Notes:	Route:			
	Distance:		Time:	
	Weight:		Speed:	
	Burn Cals:		Heart Rate:	
	Weather:		Breathing:	
	How I Felt:			
	Injuries:			
	Overall Thoughts:			

Weekly Review

Total Distance:		Weight loss:	
Average Speed:		Total Hours:	
Average Heart Rate:		Total Burns:	

Notes / Thoughts:

Year: .... Month: .... Week: .... Weekly Goal: ....

Monday	Date:	Burns Target:
Notes:	Route:	
	Distance:	Time:
	Weight:	Speed:
	Burn Cals:	Heart Rate:
	Weather:	Breathing:
	How I Felt:	
	Injuries:	
	Overall Thoughts:	

Tuesday	Date:	Burns Target:
Notes:	Route:	
	Distance:	Time:
	Weight:	Speed:
	Burn Cals:	Heart Rate:
	Weather:	Breathing:
	How I Felt:	
	Injuries:	
	Overall Thoughts:	

Wednesday	Date:	Burns Target:
Notes:	Route:	
	Distance:	Time:
	Weight:	Speed:
	Burn Cals:	Heart Rate:
	Weather:	Breathing:
	How I Felt:	
	Injuries:	
	Overall Thoughts:	

Thursday	Date:	Burns Target:
Notes:	Route:	
	Distance:	Time:
	Weight:	Speed:
	Burn Cals:	Heart Rate:
	Weather:	Breathing:
	How I Felt:	
	Injuries:	
	Overall Thoughts:	

Friday	Date:		Burns Target:	
Notes:	Route:			
	Distance:		Time:	
	Weight:		Speed:	
	Burn Cals:		Heart Rate:	
	Weather:		Breathing:	
	How I Felt:			
	Injuries:			
	Overall Thoughts:			

Saturday	Date:		Burns Target:	
Notes:	Route:			
	Distance:		Time:	
	Weight:		Speed:	
	Burn Cals:		Heart Rate:	
	Weather:		Breathing:	
	How I Felt:			
	Injuries:			
	Overall Thoughts:			

Sunday	Date:		Burns Target:	
Notes:	Route:			
	Distance:		Time:	
	Weight:		Speed:	
	Burn Cals:		Heart Rate:	
	Weather:		Breathing:	
	How I Felt:			
	Injuries:			
	Overall Thoughts:			

Weekly Review

Total Distance:		Weight loss:	
Average Speed:		Total Hours:	
Average Heart Rate:		Total Burns:	

Notes / Thoughts:

Year: _____ Month: _____ Week: _____ Weekly Goal: _____

Monday	Date:	Burns Target:
Notes:	Route:	
	Distance:	Time:
	Weight:	Speed:
	Burn Cals:	Heart Rate:
	Weather:	Breathing:
	How I Felt:	
	Injuries:	
	Overall Thoughts:	

Tuesday	Date:	Burns Target:
Notes:	Route:	
	Distance:	Time:
	Weight:	Speed:
	Burn Cals:	Heart Rate:
	Weather:	Breathing:
	How I Felt:	
	Injuries:	
	Overall Thoughts:	

Wednesday	Date:	Burns Target:
Notes:	Route:	
	Distance:	Time:
	Weight:	Speed:
	Burn Cals:	Heart Rate:
	Weather:	Breathing:
	How I Felt:	
	Injuries:	
	Overall Thoughts:	

Thursday	Date:	Burns Target:
Notes:	Route:	
	Distance:	Time:
	Weight:	Speed:
	Burn Cals:	Heart Rate:
	Weather:	Breathing:
	How I Felt:	
	Injuries:	
	Overall Thoughts:	

Friday	Date:		Burns Target:	
Notes:	Route:			
	Distance:		Time:	
	Weight:		Speed:	
	Burn Cals:		Heart Rate:	
	Weather:		Breathing:	
	How I Felt:			
	Injuries:			
	Overall Thoughts:			

Saturday	Date:		Burns Target:	
Notes:	Route:			
	Distance:		Time:	
	Weight:		Speed:	
	Burn Cals:		Heart Rate:	
	Weather:		Breathing:	
	How I Felt:			
	Injuries:			
	Overall Thoughts:			

Sunday	Date:		Burns Target:	
Notes:	Route:			
	Distance:		Time:	
	Weight:		Speed:	
	Burn Cals:		Heart Rate:	
	Weather:		Breathing:	
	How I Felt:			
	Injuries:			
	Overall Thoughts:			

Weekly Review

Total Distance:		Weight loss:	
Average Speed:		Total Hours:	
Average Heart Rate:		Total Burns:	

Notes / Thoughts:

Year:_____ Month:_____ Week:_____ Weekly Goal:_____

Monday	Date:	Burns Target:
Notes:	Route:	
	Distance:	Time:
	Weight:	Speed:
	Burn Cals:	Heart Rate:
	Weather:	Breathing:
	How I Felt:	
	Injuries:	
	Overall Thoughts:	

Tuesday	Date:	Burns Target:
Notes:	Route:	
	Distance:	Time:
	Weight:	Speed:
	Burn Cals:	Heart Rate:
	Weather:	Breathing:
	How I Felt:	
	Injuries:	
	Overall Thoughts:	

Wednesday	Date:	Burns Target:
Notes:	Route:	
	Distance:	Time:
	Weight:	Speed:
	Burn Cals:	Heart Rate:
	Weather:	Breathing:
	How I Felt:	
	Injuries:	
	Overall Thoughts:	

Thursday	Date:	Burns Target:
Notes:	Route:	
	Distance:	Time:
	Weight:	Speed:
	Burn Cals:	Heart Rate:
	Weather:	Breathing:
	How I Felt:	
	Injuries:	
	Overall Thoughts:	

Friday	Date:		Burns Target:
Notes:	Route:		
	Distance:		Time:
	Weight:		Speed:
	Burn Cals:		Heart Rate:
	Weather:		Breathing:
	How I Felt:		
	Injuries:		
	Overall Thoughts:		

Saturday	Date:		Burns Target:
Notes:	Route:		
	Distance:		Time:
	Weight:		Speed:
	Burn Cals:		Heart Rate:
	Weather:		Breathing:
	How I Felt:		
	Injuries:		
	Overall Thoughts:		

Sunday	Date:		Burns Target:
Notes:	Route:		
	Distance:		Time:
	Weight:		Speed:
	Burn Cals:		Heart Rate:
	Weather:		Breathing:
	How I Felt:		
	Injuries:		
	Overall Thoughts:		

Weekly Review

Total Distance:		Weight loss:	
Average Speed:		Total Hours:	
Average Heart Rate:		Total Burns:	

Notes / Thoughts:

Year: .... Month: .... Week: .... Weekly Goal: ....

Monday	Date:	Burns Target:

Notes:

Route:	
Distance:	Time:
Weight:	Speed:
Burn Cals:	Heart Rate:
Weather:	Breathing:
How I Felt:	
Injuries:	
Overall Thoughts:	

Tuesday	Date:	Burns Target:

Notes:

Route:	
Distance:	Time:
Weight:	Speed:
Burn Cals:	Heart Rate:
Weather:	Breathing:
How I Felt:	
Injuries:	
Overall Thoughts:	

Wednesday	Date:	Burns Target:

Notes:

Route:	
Distance:	Time:
Weight:	Speed:
Burn Cals:	Heart Rate:
Weather:	Breathing:
How I Felt:	
Injuries:	
Overall Thoughts:	

Thursday	Date:	Burns Target:

Notes:

Route:	
Distance:	Time:
Weight:	Speed:
Burn Cals:	Heart Rate:
Weather:	Breathing:
How I Felt:	
Injuries:	
Overall Thoughts:	

Friday

Date:		Burns Target:	
Notes:	Route:		
	Distance:	Time:	
	Weight:	Speed:	
	Burn Cals:	Heart Rate:	
	Weather:	Breathing:	
	How I Felt:		
	Injuries:		
	Overall Thoughts:		

Saturday

Date:		Burns Target:	
Notes:	Route:		
	Distance:	Time:	
	Weight:	Speed:	
	Burn Cals:	Heart Rate:	
	Weather:	Breathing:	
	How I Felt:		
	Injuries:		
	Overall Thoughts:		

Sunday

Date:		Burns Target:	
Notes:	Route:		
	Distance:	Time:	
	Weight:	Speed:	
	Burn Cals:	Heart Rate:	
	Weather:	Breathing:	
	How I Felt:		
	Injuries:		
	Overall Thoughts:		

Weekly Review

Total Distance:		Weight loss:	
Average Speed:		Total Hours:	
Average Heart Rate:		Total Burns:	

Notes / Thoughts:

Year:_____ Month:_____ Week:_____ Weekly Goal:_____

Monday	**Date:**		**Burns Target:**
Notes:	Route:		
	Distance:	Time:	
	Weight:	Speed:	
	Burn Cals:	Heart Rate:	
	Weather:	Breathing:	
	How I Felt:		
	Injuries:		
	Overall Thoughts:		

Tuesday	**Date:**		**Burns Target:**
Notes:	Route:		
	Distance:	Time:	
	Weight:	Speed:	
	Burn Cals:	Heart Rate:	
	Weather:	Breathing:	
	How I Felt:		
	Injuries:		
	Overall Thoughts:		

Wednesday	**Date:**		**Burns Target:**
Notes:	Route:		
	Distance:	Time:	
	Weight:	Speed:	
	Burn Cals:	Heart Rate:	
	Weather:	Breathing:	
	How I Felt:		
	Injuries:		
	Overall Thoughts:		

Thursday	**Date:**		**Burns Target:**
Notes:	Route:		
	Distance:	Time:	
	Weight:	Speed:	
	Burn Cals:	Heart Rate:	
	Weather:	Breathing:	
	How I Felt:		
	Injuries:		
	Overall Thoughts:		

Friday	Date:		Burns Target:
Notes:	Route:		
	Distance:		Time:
	Weight:		Speed:
	Burn Cals:		Heart Rate:
	Weather:		Breathing:
	How I Felt:		
	Injuries:		
	Overall Thoughts:		

Saturday	Date:		Burns Target:
Notes:	Route:		
	Distance:		Time:
	Weight:		Speed:
	Burn Cals:		Heart Rate:
	Weather:		Breathing:
	How I Felt:		
	Injuries:		
	Overall Thoughts:		

Sunday	Date:		Burns Target:
Notes:	Route:		
	Distance:		Time:
	Weight:		Speed:
	Burn Cals:		Heart Rate:
	Weather:		Breathing:
	How I Felt:		
	Injuries:		
	Overall Thoughts:		

Weekly Review

Total Distance:		Weight loss:	
Average Speed:		Total Hours:	
Average Heart Rate:		Total Burns:	

Notes / Thoughts:

Year:_____ Month:_____ Week:_____ Weekly Goal:_____

Monday	Date:	Burns Target:
Notes:	Route:	
	Distance:	Time:
	Weight:	Speed:
	Burn Cals:	Heart Rate:
	Weather:	Breathing:
	How I Felt:	
	Injuries:	
	Overall Thoughts:	

Tuesday	Date:	Burns Target:
Notes:	Route:	
	Distance:	Time:
	Weight:	Speed:
	Burn Cals:	Heart Rate:
	Weather:	Breathing:
	How I Felt:	
	Injuries:	
	Overall Thoughts:	

Wednesday	Date:	Burns Target:
Notes:	Route:	
	Distance:	Time:
	Weight:	Speed:
	Burn Cals:	Heart Rate:
	Weather:	Breathing:
	How I Felt:	
	Injuries:	
	Overall Thoughts:	

Thursday	Date:	Burns Target:
Notes:	Route:	
	Distance:	Time:
	Weight:	Speed:
	Burn Cals:	Heart Rate:
	Weather:	Breathing:
	How I Felt:	
	Injuries:	
	Overall Thoughts:	

Friday	Date:		Burns Target:	
Notes:	Route:			
	Distance:		Time:	
	Weight:		Speed:	
	Burn Cals:		Heart Rate:	
	Weather:		Breathing:	
	How I Felt:			
	Injuries:			
	Overall Thoughts:			

Saturday	Date:		Burns Target:	
Notes:	Route:			
	Distance:		Time:	
	Weight:		Speed:	
	Burn Cals:		Heart Rate:	
	Weather:		Breathing:	
	How I Felt:			
	Injuries:			
	Overall Thoughts:			

Sunday	Date:		Burns Target:	
Notes:	Route:			
	Distance:		Time:	
	Weight:		Speed:	
	Burn Cals:		Heart Rate:	
	Weather:		Breathing:	
	How I Felt:			
	Injuries:			
	Overall Thoughts:			

Weekly Review

Total Distance:		Weight loss:	
Average Speed:		Total Hours:	
Average Heart Rate:		Total Burns:	

Notes / Thoughts:

Year:_____ Month:_____ Week:_____ Weekly Goal:_____

Monday	Date:	Burns Target:
Notes:	Route:	
	Distance:	Time:
	Weight:	Speed:
	Burn Cals:	Heart Rate:
	Weather:	Breathing:
	How I Felt:	
	Injuries:	
	Overall Thoughts:	

Tuesday	Date:	Burns Target:
Notes:	Route:	
	Distance:	Time:
	Weight:	Speed:
	Burn Cals:	Heart Rate:
	Weather:	Breathing:
	How I Felt:	
	Injuries:	
	Overall Thoughts:	

Wednesday	Date:	Burns Target:
Notes:	Route:	
	Distance:	Time:
	Weight:	Speed:
	Burn Cals:	Heart Rate:
	Weather:	Breathing:
	How I Felt:	
	Injuries:	
	Overall Thoughts:	

Thursday	Date:	Burns Target:
Notes:	Route:	
	Distance:	Time:
	Weight:	Speed:
	Burn Cals:	Heart Rate:
	Weather:	Breathing:
	How I Felt:	
	Injuries:	
	Overall Thoughts:	

Friday	Date:		Burns Target:	
Notes:	Route:			
	Distance:		Time:	
	Weight:		Speed:	
	Burn Cals:		Heart Rate:	
	Weather:		Breathing:	
	How I Felt:			
	Injuries:			
	Overall Thoughts:			

Saturday	Date:		Burns Target:	
Notes:	Route:			
	Distance:		Time:	
	Weight:		Speed:	
	Burn Cals:		Heart Rate:	
	Weather:		Breathing:	
	How I Felt:			
	Injuries:			
	Overall Thoughts:			

Sunday	Date:		Burns Target:	
Notes:	Route:			
	Distance:		Time:	
	Weight:		Speed:	
	Burn Cals:		Heart Rate:	
	Weather:		Breathing:	
	How I Felt:			
	Injuries:			
	Overall Thoughts:			

Weekly Review

Total Distance:		Weight loss:	
Average Speed:		Total Hours:	
Average Heart Rate:		Total Burns:	

Notes / Thoughts:

Year: _____ Month: _____ Week: _____ Weekly Goal: _____

Monday	Date:		Burns Target:
Notes:	Route:		
	Distance:		Time:
	Weight:		Speed:
	Burn Cals:		Heart Rate:
	Weather:		Breathing:
	How I Felt:		
	Injuries:		
	Overall Thoughts:		

Tuesday	Date:		Burns Target:
Notes:	Route:		
	Distance:		Time:
	Weight:		Speed:
	Burn Cals:		Heart Rate:
	Weather:		Breathing:
	How I Felt:		
	Injuries:		
	Overall Thoughts:		

Wednesday	Date:		Burns Target:
Notes:	Route:		
	Distance:		Time:
	Weight:		Speed:
	Burn Cals:		Heart Rate:
	Weather:		Breathing:
	How I Felt:		
	Injuries:		
	Overall Thoughts:		

Thursday	Date:		Burns Target:
Notes:	Route:		
	Distance:		Time:
	Weight:		Speed:
	Burn Cals:		Heart Rate:
	Weather:		Breathing:
	How I Felt:		
	Injuries:		
	Overall Thoughts:		

Friday	Date:		Burns Target:
Notes:	Route:		
	Distance:		Time:
	Weight:		Speed:
	Burn Cals:		Heart Rate:
	Weather:		Breathing:
	How I Felt:		
	Injuries:		
	Overall Thoughts:		

Saturday	Date:		Burns Target:
Notes:	Route:		
	Distance:		Time:
	Weight:		Speed:
	Burn Cals:		Heart Rate:
	Weather:		Breathing:
	How I Felt:		
	Injuries:		
	Overall Thoughts:		

Sunday	Date:		Burns Target:
Notes:	Route:		
	Distance:		Time:
	Weight:		Speed:
	Burn Cals:		Heart Rate:
	Weather:		Breathing:
	How I Felt:		
	Injuries:		
	Overall Thoughts:		

Weekly Review

Total Distance:		Weight loss:	
Average Speed:		Total Hours:	
Average Heart Rate:		Total Burns:	

Notes / Thoughts:

Year:_____ Month:_____ Week:_____ Weekly Goal:_____

Monday	Date:		Burns Target:
Notes:	Route:		
	Distance:		Time:
	Weight:		Speed:
	Burn Cals:		Heart Rate:
	Weather:		Breathing:
	How I Felt:		
	Injuries:		
	Overall Thoughts:		

Tuesday	Date:		Burns Target:
Notes:	Route:		
	Distance:		Time:
	Weight:		Speed:
	Burn Cals:		Heart Rate:
	Weather:		Breathing:
	How I Felt:		
	Injuries:		
	Overall Thoughts:		

Wednesday	Date:		Burns Target:
Notes:	Route:		
	Distance:		Time:
	Weight:		Speed:
	Burn Cals:		Heart Rate:
	Weather:		Breathing:
	How I Felt:		
	Injuries:		
	Overall Thoughts:		

Thursday	Date:		Burns Target:
Notes:	Route:		
	Distance:		Time:
	Weight:		Speed:
	Burn Cals:		Heart Rate:
	Weather:		Breathing:
	How I Felt:		
	Injuries:		
	Overall Thoughts:		

Friday	Date:		Burns Target:
Notes:	Route:		
	Distance:	Time:	
	Weight:	Speed:	
	Burn Cals:	Heart Rate:	
	Weather:	Breathing:	
	How I Felt:		
	Injuries:		
	Overall Thoughts:		

Saturday	Date:		Burns Target:
Notes:	Route:		
	Distance:	Time:	
	Weight:	Speed:	
	Burn Cals:	Heart Rate:	
	Weather:	Breathing:	
	How I Felt:		
	Injuries:		
	Overall Thoughts:		

Sunday	Date:		Burns Target:
Notes:	Route:		
	Distance:	Time:	
	Weight:	Speed:	
	Burn Cals:	Heart Rate:	
	Weather:	Breathing:	
	How I Felt:		
	Injuries:		
	Overall Thoughts:		

Weekly Review

Total Distance:		Weight loss:	
Average Speed:		Total Hours:	
Average Heart Rate:		Total Burns:	

Notes / Thoughts:

Year:............ Month:............ Week:............ Weekly Goal:..........

Monday	Date:	Burns Target:		
Notes:	Route:			
	Distance:		Time:	
	Weight:		Speed:	
	Burn Cals:		Heart Rate:	
	Weather:		Breathing:	
	How I Felt:			
	Injuries:			
	Overall Thoughts:			

Tuesday	Date:	Burns Target:		
Notes:	Route:			
	Distance:		Time:	
	Weight:		Speed:	
	Burn Cals:		Heart Rate:	
	Weather:		Breathing:	
	How I Felt:			
	Injuries:			
	Overall Thoughts:			

Wednesday	Date:	Burns Target:		
Notes:	Route:			
	Distance:		Time:	
	Weight:		Speed:	
	Burn Cals:		Heart Rate:	
	Weather:		Breathing:	
	How I Felt:			
	Injuries:			
	Overall Thoughts:			

Thursday	Date:	Burns Target:		
Notes:	Route:			
	Distance:		Time:	
	Weight:		Speed:	
	Burn Cals:		Heart Rate:	
	Weather:		Breathing:	
	How I Felt:			
	Injuries:			
	Overall Thoughts:			

Friday	Date:		Burns Target:
Notes:	Route:		
	Distance:		Time:
	Weight:		Speed:
	Burn Cals:		Heart Rate:
	Weather:		Breathing:
	How I Felt:		
	Injuries:		
	Overall Thoughts:		

Saturday	Date:		Burns Target:
Notes:	Route:		
	Distance:		Time:
	Weight:		Speed:
	Burn Cals:		Heart Rate:
	Weather:		Breathing:
	How I Felt:		
	Injuries:		
	Overall Thoughts:		

Sunday	Date:		Burns Target:
Notes:	Route:		
	Distance:		Time:
	Weight:		Speed:
	Burn Cals:		Heart Rate:
	Weather:		Breathing:
	How I Felt:		
	Injuries:		
	Overall Thoughts:		

Weekly Review

Total Distance:		Weight loss:	
Average Speed:		Total Hours:	
Average Heart Rate:		Total Burns:	

Notes / Thoughts:

Year:.............. Month:.............. Week: .... Weekly Goal: ....

Monday	Date:		Burns Target:
Notes:	Route:		
	Distance:		Time:
	Weight:		Speed:
	Burn Cals:		Heart Rate:
	Weather:		Breathing:
	How I Felt:		
	Injuries:		
	Overall Thoughts:		

Tuesday	Date:		Burns Target:
Notes:	Route:		
	Distance:		Time:
	Weight:		Speed:
	Burn Cals:		Heart Rate:
	Weather:		Breathing:
	How I Felt:		
	Injuries:		
	Overall Thoughts:		

Wednesday	Date:		Burns Target:
Notes:	Route:		
	Distance:		Time:
	Weight:		Speed:
	Burn Cals:		Heart Rate:
	Weather:		Breathing:
	How I Felt:		
	Injuries:		
	Overall Thoughts:		

Thursday	Date:		Burns Target:
Notes:	Route:		
	Distance:		Time:
	Weight:		Speed:
	Burn Cals:		Heart Rate:
	Weather:		Breathing:
	How I Felt:		
	Injuries:		
	Overall Thoughts:		

Friday	Date:		Burns Target:
Notes:	Route:		
	Distance:		Time:
	Weight:		Speed:
	Burn Cals:		Heart Rate:
	Weather:		Breathing:
	How I Felt:		
	Injuries:		
	Overall Thoughts:		

Saturday	Date:		Burns Target:
Notes:	Route:		
	Distance:		Time:
	Weight:		Speed:
	Burn Cals:		Heart Rate:
	Weather:		Breathing:
	How I Felt:		
	Injuries:		
	Overall Thoughts:		

Sunday	Date:		Burns Target:
Notes:	Route:		
	Distance:		Time:
	Weight:		Speed:
	Burn Cals:		Heart Rate:
	Weather:		Breathing:
	How I Felt:		
	Injuries:		
	Overall Thoughts:		

Weekly Review			
Total Distance:		Weight loss:	
Average Speed:		Total Hours:	
Average Heart Rate:		Total Burns:	
Notes / Thoughts:			

Year:............ Month:............ Week: .... Weekly Goal: ....

Monday	Date:	Burns Target:
Notes:	Route:	
	Distance:	Time:
	Weight:	Speed:
	Burn Cals:	Heart Rate:
	Weather:	Breathing:
	How I Felt:	
	Injuries:	
	Overall Thoughts:	

Tuesday	Date:	Burns Target:
Notes:	Route:	
	Distance:	Time:
	Weight:	Speed:
	Burn Cals:	Heart Rate:
	Weather:	Breathing:
	How I Felt:	
	Injuries:	
	Overall Thoughts:	

Wednesday	Date:	Burns Target:
Notes:	Route:	
	Distance:	Time:
	Weight:	Speed:
	Burn Cals:	Heart Rate:
	Weather:	Breathing:
	How I Felt:	
	Injuries:	
	Overall Thoughts:	

Thursday	Date:	Burns Target:
Notes:	Route:	
	Distance:	Time:
	Weight:	Speed:
	Burn Cals:	Heart Rate:
	Weather:	Breathing:
	How I Felt:	
	Injuries:	
	Overall Thoughts:	

Friday	Date:		Burns Target:	
Notes:	Route:			
	Distance:		Time:	
	Weight:		Speed:	
	Burn Cals:		Heart Rate:	
	Weather:		Breathing:	
	How I Felt:			
	Injuries:			
	Overall Thoughts:			

Saturday	Date:		Burns Target:	
Notes:	Route:			
	Distance:		Time:	
	Weight:		Speed:	
	Burn Cals:		Heart Rate:	
	Weather:		Breathing:	
	How I Felt:			
	Injuries:			
	Overall Thoughts:			

Sunday	Date:		Burns Target:	
Notes:	Route:			
	Distance:		Time:	
	Weight:		Speed:	
	Burn Cals:		Heart Rate:	
	Weather:		Breathing:	
	How I Felt:			
	Injuries:			
	Overall Thoughts:			

Weekly Review

Total Distance:		Weight loss:	
Average Speed:		Total Hours:	
Average Heart Rate:		Total Burns:	

Notes / Thoughts:

Year:_____ Month:_____ Week:_____ Weekly Goal:_____

Monday	**Date:**	**Burns Target:**

Notes:

Route:
Distance: Time:
Weight: Speed:
Burn Cals: Heart Rate:
Weather: Breathing:
How I Felt:
Injuries:
Overall Thoughts:

Tuesday	**Date:**	**Burns Target:**

Notes:

Route:
Distance: Time:
Weight: Speed:
Burn Cals: Heart Rate:
Weather: Breathing:
How I Felt:
Injuries:
Overall Thoughts:

Wednesday	**Date:**	**Burns Target:**

Notes:

Route:
Distance: Time:
Weight: Speed:
Burn Cals: Heart Rate:
Weather: Breathing:
How I Felt:
Injuries:
Overall Thoughts:

Thursday	**Date:**	**Burns Target:**

Notes:

Route:
Distance: Time:
Weight: Speed:
Burn Cals: Heart Rate:
Weather: Breathing:
How I Felt:
Injuries:
Overall Thoughts:

Friday	Date:		Burns Target:
Notes:	Route:		
	Distance:		Time:
	Weight:		Speed:
	Burn Cals:		Heart Rate:
	Weather:		Breathing:
	How I Felt:		
	Injuries:		
	Overall Thoughts:		

Saturday	Date:		Burns Target:
Notes:	Route:		
	Distance:		Time:
	Weight:		Speed:
	Burn Cals:		Heart Rate:
	Weather:		Breathing:
	How I Felt:		
	Injuries:		
	Overall Thoughts:		

Sunday	Date:		Burns Target:
Notes:	Route:		
	Distance:		Time:
	Weight:		Speed:
	Burn Cals:		Heart Rate:
	Weather:		Breathing:
	How I Felt:		
	Injuries:		
	Overall Thoughts:		

Weekly Review

Total Distance:		Weight loss:	
Average Speed:		Total Hours:	
Average Heart Rate:		Total Burns:	

Notes / Thoughts:

Year:.............. Month:.............. Week:.............. Weekly Goal:..........

Monday | Date: | Burns Target:

Monday	Date:		Burns Target:
Notes:	Route:		
	Distance:	Time:	
	Weight:	Speed:	
	Burn Cals:	Heart Rate:	
	Weather:	Breathing:	
	How I Felt:		
	Injuries:		
	Overall Thoughts:		

Tuesday	Date:		Burns Target:
Notes:	Route:		
	Distance:	Time:	
	Weight:	Speed:	
	Burn Cals:	Heart Rate:	
	Weather:	Breathing:	
	How I Felt:		
	Injuries:		
	Overall Thoughts:		

Wednesday	Date:		Burns Target:
Notes:	Route:		
	Distance:	Time:	
	Weight:	Speed:	
	Burn Cals:	Heart Rate:	
	Weather:	Breathing:	
	How I Felt:		
	Injuries:		
	Overall Thoughts:		

Thursday	Date:		Burns Target:
Notes:	Route:		
	Distance:	Time:	
	Weight:	Speed:	
	Burn Cals:	Heart Rate:	
	Weather:	Breathing:	
	How I Felt:		
	Injuries:		
	Overall Thoughts:		

Friday	Date:		Burns Target:	
Notes:	Route:			
	Distance:		Time:	
	Weight:		Speed:	
	Burn Cals:		Heart Rate:	
	Weather:		Breathing:	
	How I Felt:			
	Injuries:			
	Overall Thoughts:			

Saturday	Date:		Burns Target:	
Notes:	Route:			
	Distance:		Time:	
	Weight:		Speed:	
	Burn Cals:		Heart Rate:	
	Weather:		Breathing:	
	How I Felt:			
	Injuries:			
	Overall Thoughts:			

Sunday	Date:		Burns Target:	
Notes:	Route:			
	Distance:		Time:	
	Weight:		Speed:	
	Burn Cals:		Heart Rate:	
	Weather:		Breathing:	
	How I Felt:			
	Injuries:			
	Overall Thoughts:			

Weekly Review

Total Distance:		Weight loss:	
Average Speed:		Total Hours:	
Average Heart Rate:		Total Burns:	

Notes / Thoughts:

Year:_____ Month:_____ Week: _____ Weekly Goal: _____

Monday	Date:		Burns Target:
Notes:	Route:		
	Distance:	Time:	
	Weight:	Speed:	
	Burn Cals:	Heart Rate:	
	Weather:	Breathing:	
	How I Felt:		
	Injuries:		
	Overall Thoughts:		

Tuesday	Date:		Burns Target:
Notes:	Route:		
	Distance:	Time:	
	Weight:	Speed:	
	Burn Cals:	Heart Rate:	
	Weather:	Breathing:	
	How I Felt:		
	Injuries:		
	Overall Thoughts:		

Wednesday	Date:		Burns Target:
Notes:	Route:		
	Distance:	Time:	
	Weight:	Speed:	
	Burn Cals:	Heart Rate:	
	Weather:	Breathing:	
	How I Felt:		
	Injuries:		
	Overall Thoughts:		

Thursday	Date:		Burns Target:
Notes:	Route:		
	Distance:	Time:	
	Weight:	Speed:	
	Burn Cals:	Heart Rate:	
	Weather:	Breathing:	
	How I Felt:		
	Injuries:		
	Overall Thoughts:		

Friday	Date:		Burns Target:
Notes:	Route:		
	Distance:		Time:
	Weight:		Speed:
	Burn Cals:		Heart Rate:
	Weather:		Breathing:
	How I Felt:		
	Injuries:		
	Overall Thoughts:		

Saturday	Date:		Burns Target:
Notes:	Route:		
	Distance:		Time:
	Weight:		Speed:
	Burn Cals:		Heart Rate:
	Weather:		Breathing:
	How I Felt:		
	Injuries:		
	Overall Thoughts:		

Sunday	Date:		Burns Target:
Notes:	Route:		
	Distance:		Time:
	Weight:		Speed:
	Burn Cals:		Heart Rate:
	Weather:		Breathing:
	How I Felt:		
	Injuries:		
	Overall Thoughts:		

Weekly Review			
Total Distance:		Weight loss:	
Average Speed:		Total Hours:	
Average Heart Rate:		Total Burns:	
Notes / Thoughts:			

Year:_____ Month:_____ Week:_____ Weekly Goal:_____

Monday	**Date:**	**Burns Target:**
Notes:	Route:	
	Distance:	Time:
	Weight:	Speed:
	Burn Cals:	Heart Rate:
	Weather:	Breathing:
	How I Felt:	
	Injuries:	
	Overall Thoughts:	

Tuesday	**Date:**	**Burns Target:**
Notes:	Route:	
	Distance:	Time:
	Weight:	Speed:
	Burn Cals:	Heart Rate:
	Weather:	Breathing:
	How I Felt:	
	Injuries:	
	Overall Thoughts:	

Wednesday	**Date:**	**Burns Target:**
Notes:	Route:	
	Distance:	Time:
	Weight:	Speed:
	Burn Cals:	Heart Rate:
	Weather:	Breathing:
	How I Felt:	
	Injuries:	
	Overall Thoughts:	

Thursday	**Date:**	**Burns Target:**
Notes:	Route:	
	Distance:	Time:
	Weight:	Speed:
	Burn Cals:	Heart Rate:
	Weather:	Breathing:
	How I Felt:	
	Injuries:	
	Overall Thoughts:	

Friday	**Date:**		**Burns Target:**
Notes:	Route:		
	Distance:		Time:
	Weight:		Speed:
	Burn Cals:		Heart Rate:
	Weather:		Breathing:
	How I Felt:		
	Injuries:		
	Overall Thoughts:		

Saturday	**Date:**		**Burns Target:**
Notes:	Route:		
	Distance:		Time:
	Weight:		Speed:
	Burn Cals:		Heart Rate:
	Weather:		Breathing:
	How I Felt:		
	Injuries:		
	Overall Thoughts:		

Sunday	**Date:**		**Burns Target:**
Notes:	Route:		
	Distance:		Time:
	Weight:		Speed:
	Burn Cals:		Heart Rate:
	Weather:		Breathing:
	How I Felt:		
	Injuries:		
	Overall Thoughts:		

Weekly Review

Total Distance:		Weight loss:	
Average Speed:		Total Hours:	
Average Heart Rate:		Total Burns:	

Notes / Thoughts:

Year: _____ Month: _____ Week: _____ Weekly Goal: _____

Monday	Date:	Burns Target:	
Notes:	Route:		
	Distance:	Time:	
	Weight:	Speed:	
	Burn Cals:	Heart Rate:	
	Weather:	Breathing:	
	How I Felt:		
	Injuries:		
	Overall Thoughts:		

Tuesday	Date:	Burns Target:	
Notes:	Route:		
	Distance:	Time:	
	Weight:	Speed:	
	Burn Cals:	Heart Rate:	
	Weather:	Breathing:	
	How I Felt:		
	Injuries:		
	Overall Thoughts:		

Wednesday	Date:	Burns Target:	
Notes:	Route:		
	Distance:	Time:	
	Weight:	Speed:	
	Burn Cals:	Heart Rate:	
	Weather:	Breathing:	
	How I Felt:		
	Injuries:		
	Overall Thoughts:		

Thursday	Date:	Burns Target:	
Notes:	Route:		
	Distance:	Time:	
	Weight:	Speed:	
	Burn Cals:	Heart Rate:	
	Weather:	Breathing:	
	How I Felt:		
	Injuries:		
	Overall Thoughts:		

Friday	Date:		Burns Target:	
Notes:	Route:			
	Distance:		Time:	
	Weight:		Speed:	
	Burn Cals:		Heart Rate:	
	Weather:		Breathing:	
	How I Felt:			
	Injuries:			
	Overall Thoughts:			

Saturday	Date:		Burns Target:	
Notes:	Route:			
	Distance:		Time:	
	Weight:		Speed:	
	Burn Cals:		Heart Rate:	
	Weather:		Breathing:	
	How I Felt:			
	Injuries:			
	Overall Thoughts:			

Sunday	Date:		Burns Target:	
Notes:	Route:			
	Distance:		Time:	
	Weight:		Speed:	
	Burn Cals:		Heart Rate:	
	Weather:		Breathing:	
	How I Felt:			
	Injuries:			
	Overall Thoughts:			

Weekly Review

Total Distance:		Weight loss:	
Average Speed:		Total Hours:	
Average Heart Rate:		Total Burns:	

Notes / Thoughts:

Year: _____ Month: _____ Week: _____ Weekly Goal: _____

Monday	Date:	Burns Target:
Notes:	Route:	
	Distance:	Time:
	Weight:	Speed:
	Burn Cals:	Heart Rate:
	Weather:	Breathing:
	How I Felt:	
	Injuries:	
	Overall Thoughts:	

Tuesday	Date:	Burns Target:
Notes:	Route:	
	Distance:	Time:
	Weight:	Speed:
	Burn Cals:	Heart Rate:
	Weather:	Breathing:
	How I Felt:	
	Injuries:	
	Overall Thoughts:	

Wednesday	Date:	Burns Target:
Notes:	Route:	
	Distance:	Time:
	Weight:	Speed:
	Burn Cals:	Heart Rate:
	Weather:	Breathing:
	How I Felt:	
	Injuries:	
	Overall Thoughts:	

Thursday	Date:	Burns Target:
Notes:	Route:	
	Distance:	Time:
	Weight:	Speed:
	Burn Cals:	Heart Rate:
	Weather:	Breathing:
	How I Felt:	
	Injuries:	
	Overall Thoughts:	

Friday

Friday	Date:		Burns Target:

Notes:

Route:	
Distance:	Time:
Weight:	Speed:
Burn Cals:	Heart Rate:
Weather:	Breathing:
How I Felt:	
Injuries:	
Overall Thoughts:	

Saturday

Saturday	Date:		Burns Target:

Notes:

Route:	
Distance:	Time:
Weight:	Speed:
Burn Cals:	Heart Rate:
Weather:	Breathing:
How I Felt:	
Injuries:	
Overall Thoughts:	

Sunday

Sunday	Date:		Burns Target:

Notes:

Route:	
Distance:	Time:
Weight:	Speed:
Burn Cals:	Heart Rate:
Weather:	Breathing:
How I Felt:	
Injuries:	
Overall Thoughts:	

Weekly Review

Total Distance:		Weight loss:	
Average Speed:		Total Hours:	
Average Heart Rate:		Total Burns:	

Notes / Thoughts:

Year: _____ Month: _____ Week: _____ Weekly Goal: _____

Monday	Date:	Burns Target:
Notes:	Route:	
	Distance:	Time:
	Weight:	Speed:
	Burn Cals:	Heart Rate:
	Weather:	Breathing:
	How I Felt:	
	Injuries:	
	Overall Thoughts:	

Tuesday	Date:	Burns Target:
Notes:	Route:	
	Distance:	Time:
	Weight:	Speed:
	Burn Cals:	Heart Rate:
	Weather:	Breathing:
	How I Felt:	
	Injuries:	
	Overall Thoughts:	

Wednesday	Date:	Burns Target:
Notes:	Route:	
	Distance:	Time:
	Weight:	Speed:
	Burn Cals:	Heart Rate:
	Weather:	Breathing:
	How I Felt:	
	Injuries:	
	Overall Thoughts:	

Thursday	Date:	Burns Target:
Notes:	Route:	
	Distance:	Time:
	Weight:	Speed:
	Burn Cals:	Heart Rate:
	Weather:	Breathing:
	How I Felt:	
	Injuries:	
	Overall Thoughts:	

Friday	Date:		Burns Target:	
Notes:	Route:			
	Distance:		Time:	
	Weight:		Speed:	
	Burn Cals:		Heart Rate:	
	Weather:		Breathing:	
	How I Felt:			
	Injuries:			
	Overall Thoughts:			

Saturday	Date:		Burns Target:	
Notes:	Route:			
	Distance:		Time:	
	Weight:		Speed:	
	Burn Cals:		Heart Rate:	
	Weather:		Breathing:	
	How I Felt:			
	Injuries:			
	Overall Thoughts:			

Sunday	Date:		Burns Target:	
Notes:	Route:			
	Distance:		Time:	
	Weight:		Speed:	
	Burn Cals:		Heart Rate:	
	Weather:		Breathing:	
	How I Felt:			
	Injuries:			
	Overall Thoughts:			

Weekly Review

Total Distance:		Weight loss:	
Average Speed:		Total Hours:	
Average Heart Rate:		Total Burns:	

Notes / Thoughts:

Year: _____ Month: _____ Week: _____ Weekly Goal: _____

Monday	Date:	Burns Target:
Notes:	Route:	
	Distance:	Time:
	Weight:	Speed:
	Burn Cals:	Heart Rate:
	Weather:	Breathing:
	How I Felt:	
	Injuries:	
	Overall Thoughts:	

Tuesday	Date:	Burns Target:
Notes:	Route:	
	Distance:	Time:
	Weight:	Speed:
	Burn Cals:	Heart Rate:
	Weather:	Breathing:
	How I Felt:	
	Injuries:	
	Overall Thoughts:	

Wednesday	Date:	Burns Target:
Notes:	Route:	
	Distance:	Time:
	Weight:	Speed:
	Burn Cals:	Heart Rate:
	Weather:	Breathing:
	How I Felt:	
	Injuries:	
	Overall Thoughts:	

Thursday	Date:	Burns Target:
Notes:	Route:	
	Distance:	Time:
	Weight:	Speed:
	Burn Cals:	Heart Rate:
	Weather:	Breathing:
	How I Felt:	
	Injuries:	
	Overall Thoughts:	

Friday

Date:		Burns Target:	
Notes:	Route:		
	Distance:	Time:	
	Weight:	Speed:	
	Burn Cals:	Heart Rate:	
	Weather:	Breathing:	
	How I Felt:		
	Injuries:		
	Overall Thoughts:		

Saturday

Date:		Burns Target:	
Notes:	Route:		
	Distance:	Time:	
	Weight:	Speed:	
	Burn Cals:	Heart Rate:	
	Weather:	Breathing:	
	How I Felt:		
	Injuries:		
	Overall Thoughts:		

Sunday

Date:		Burns Target:	
Notes:	Route:		
	Distance:	Time:	
	Weight:	Speed:	
	Burn Cals:	Heart Rate:	
	Weather:	Breathing:	
	How I Felt:		
	Injuries:		
	Overall Thoughts:		

Weekly Review

Total Distance:		Weight loss:	
Average Speed:		Total Hours:	
Average Heart Rate:		Total Burns:	

Notes / Thoughts:

Year:_____ Month:_____ Week:_____ Weekly Goal:_____

Monday	Date:	Burns Target:
Notes:	Route:	
	Distance:	Time:
	Weight:	Speed:
	Burn Cals:	Heart Rate:
	Weather:	Breathing:
	How I Felt:	
	Injuries:	
	Overall Thoughts:	

Tuesday	Date:	Burns Target:
Notes:	Route:	
	Distance:	Time:
	Weight:	Speed:
	Burn Cals:	Heart Rate:
	Weather:	Breathing:
	How I Felt:	
	Injuries:	
	Overall Thoughts:	

Wednesday	Date:	Burns Target:
Notes:	Route:	
	Distance:	Time:
	Weight:	Speed:
	Burn Cals:	Heart Rate:
	Weather:	Breathing:
	How I Felt:	
	Injuries:	
	Overall Thoughts:	

Thursday	Date:	Burns Target:
Notes:	Route:	
	Distance:	Time:
	Weight:	Speed:
	Burn Cals:	Heart Rate:
	Weather:	Breathing:
	How I Felt:	
	Injuries:	
	Overall Thoughts:	

Friday	Date:		Burns Target:	
Notes:	Route:			
	Distance:		Time:	
	Weight:		Speed:	
	Burn Cals:		Heart Rate:	
	Weather:		Breathing:	
	How I Felt:			
	Injuries:			
	Overall Thoughts:			

Saturday	Date:		Burns Target:	
Notes:	Route:			
	Distance:		Time:	
	Weight:		Speed:	
	Burn Cals:		Heart Rate:	
	Weather:		Breathing:	
	How I Felt:			
	Injuries:			
	Overall Thoughts:			

Sunday	Date:		Burns Target:	
Notes:	Route:			
	Distance:		Time:	
	Weight:		Speed:	
	Burn Cals:		Heart Rate:	
	Weather:		Breathing:	
	How I Felt:			
	Injuries:			
	Overall Thoughts:			

Weekly Review

Total Distance:		Weight loss:	
Average Speed:		Total Hours:	
Average Heart Rate:		Total Burns:	

Notes / Thoughts:

Year: .... Month: .... Week: .... Weekly Goal: ....

Monday	Date:	Burns Target:
Notes:	Route:	
	Distance:	Time:
	Weight:	Speed:
	Burn Cals:	Heart Rate:
	Weather:	Breathing:
	How I Felt:	
	Injuries:	
	Overall Thoughts:	

Tuesday	Date:	Burns Target:
Notes:	Route:	
	Distance:	Time:
	Weight:	Speed:
	Burn Cals:	Heart Rate:
	Weather:	Breathing:
	How I Felt:	
	Injuries:	
	Overall Thoughts:	

Wednesday	Date:	Burns Target:
Notes:	Route:	
	Distance:	Time:
	Weight:	Speed:
	Burn Cals:	Heart Rate:
	Weather:	Breathing:
	How I Felt:	
	Injuries:	
	Overall Thoughts:	

Thursday	Date:	Burns Target:
Notes:	Route:	
	Distance:	Time:
	Weight:	Speed:
	Burn Cals:	Heart Rate:
	Weather:	Breathing:
	How I Felt:	
	Injuries:	
	Overall Thoughts:	

Friday	Date:		Burns Target:	
Notes:	Route:			
	Distance:		Time:	
	Weight:		Speed:	
	Burn Cals:		Heart Rate:	
	Weather:		Breathing:	
	How I Felt:			
	Injuries:			
	Overall Thoughts:			

Saturday	Date:		Burns Target:	
Notes:	Route:			
	Distance:		Time:	
	Weight:		Speed:	
	Burn Cals:		Heart Rate:	
	Weather:		Breathing:	
	How I Felt:			
	Injuries:			
	Overall Thoughts:			

Sunday	Date:		Burns Target:	
Notes:	Route:			
	Distance:		Time:	
	Weight:		Speed:	
	Burn Cals:		Heart Rate:	
	Weather:		Breathing:	
	How I Felt:			
	Injuries:			
	Overall Thoughts:			

Weekly Review

Total Distance:		Weight loss:	
Average Speed:		Total Hours:	
Average Heart Rate:		Total Burns:	

Notes / Thoughts:

Year: _____ Month: _____ Week: _____ Weekly Goal: _____

Monday	Date:	Burns Target:
Notes:	Route:	
	Distance:	Time:
	Weight:	Speed:
	Burn Cals:	Heart Rate:
	Weather:	Breathing:
	How I Felt:	
	Injuries:	
	Overall Thoughts:	

Tuesday	Date:	Burns Target:
Notes:	Route:	
	Distance:	Time:
	Weight:	Speed:
	Burn Cals:	Heart Rate:
	Weather:	Breathing:
	How I Felt:	
	Injuries:	
	Overall Thoughts:	

Wednesday	Date:	Burns Target:
Notes:	Route:	
	Distance:	Time:
	Weight:	Speed:
	Burn Cals:	Heart Rate:
	Weather:	Breathing:
	How I Felt:	
	Injuries:	
	Overall Thoughts:	

Thursday	Date:	Burns Target:
Notes:	Route:	
	Distance:	Time:
	Weight:	Speed:
	Burn Cals:	Heart Rate:
	Weather:	Breathing:
	How I Felt:	
	Injuries:	
	Overall Thoughts:	

Friday	Date:		Burns Target:
Notes:	Route:		
	Distance:		Time:
	Weight:		Speed:
	Burn Cals:		Heart Rate:
	Weather:		Breathing:
	How I Felt:		
	Injuries:		
	Overall Thoughts:		

Saturday	Date:		Burns Target:
Notes:	Route:		
	Distance:		Time:
	Weight:		Speed:
	Burn Cals:		Heart Rate:
	Weather:		Breathing:
	How I Felt:		
	Injuries:		
	Overall Thoughts:		

Sunday	Date:		Burns Target:
Notes:	Route:		
	Distance:		Time:
	Weight:		Speed:
	Burn Cals:		Heart Rate:
	Weather:		Breathing:
	How I Felt:		
	Injuries:		
	Overall Thoughts:		

Weekly Review			
Total Distance:		Weight loss:	
Average Speed:		Total Hours:	
Average Heart Rate:		Total Burns:	
Notes / Thoughts:			

Year:_____ Month:_____ Week:_____ Weekly Goal:_____

Monday	**Date:**	**Burns Target:**
Notes:	Route:	
	Distance:	Time:
	Weight:	Speed:
	Burn Cals:	Heart Rate:
	Weather:	Breathing:
	How I Felt:	
	Injuries:	
	Overall Thoughts:	

Tuesday	**Date:**	**Burns Target:**
Notes:	Route:	
	Distance:	Time:
	Weight:	Speed:
	Burn Cals:	Heart Rate:
	Weather:	Breathing:
	How I Felt:	
	Injuries:	
	Overall Thoughts:	

Wednesday	**Date:**	**Burns Target:**
Notes:	Route:	
	Distance:	Time:
	Weight:	Speed:
	Burn Cals:	Heart Rate:
	Weather:	Breathing:
	How I Felt:	
	Injuries:	
	Overall Thoughts:	

Thursday	**Date:**	**Burns Target:**
Notes:	Route:	
	Distance:	Time:
	Weight:	Speed:
	Burn Cals:	Heart Rate:
	Weather:	Breathing:
	How I Felt:	
	Injuries:	
	Overall Thoughts:	

Friday	Date:		Burns Target:
Notes:	Route:		
	Distance:		Time:
	Weight:		Speed:
	Burn Cals:		Heart Rate:
	Weather:		Breathing:
	How I Felt:		
	Injuries:		
	Overall Thoughts:		

Saturday	Date:		Burns Target:
Notes:	Route:		
	Distance:		Time:
	Weight:		Speed:
	Burn Cals:		Heart Rate:
	Weather:		Breathing:
	How I Felt:		
	Injuries:		
	Overall Thoughts:		

Sunday	Date:		Burns Target:
Notes:	Route:		
	Distance:		Time:
	Weight:		Speed:
	Burn Cals:		Heart Rate:
	Weather:		Breathing:
	How I Felt:		
	Injuries:		
	Overall Thoughts:		

Weekly Review

Total Distance:		Weight loss:	
Average Speed:		Total Hours:	
Average Heart Rate:		Total Burns:	

Notes / Thoughts:

Year:_____ Month:_____ Week:_____ Weekly Goal:_____

Monday	Date:		Burns Target:
Notes:	Route:		
	Distance:		Time:
	Weight:		Speed:
	Burn Cals:		Heart Rate:
	Weather:		Breathing:
	How I Felt:		
	Injuries:		
	Overall Thoughts:		

Tuesday	Date:		Burns Target:
Notes:	Route:		
	Distance:		Time:
	Weight:		Speed:
	Burn Cals:		Heart Rate:
	Weather:		Breathing:
	How I Felt:		
	Injuries:		
	Overall Thoughts:		

Wednesday	Date:		Burns Target:
Notes:	Route:		
	Distance:		Time:
	Weight:		Speed:
	Burn Cals:		Heart Rate:
	Weather:		Breathing:
	How I Felt:		
	Injuries:		
	Overall Thoughts:		

Thursday	Date:		Burns Target:
Notes:	Route:		
	Distance:		Time:
	Weight:		Speed:
	Burn Cals:		Heart Rate:
	Weather:		Breathing:
	How I Felt:		
	Injuries:		
	Overall Thoughts:		

Friday	Date:			Burns Target:	
Notes:	Route:				
	Distance:		Time:		
	Weight:		Speed:		
	Burn Cals:		Heart Rate:		
	Weather:		Breathing:		
	How I Felt:				
	Injuries:				
	Overall Thoughts:				

Saturday	Date:			Burns Target:	
Notes:	Route:				
	Distance:		Time:		
	Weight:		Speed:		
	Burn Cals:		Heart Rate:		
	Weather:		Breathing:		
	How I Felt:				
	Injuries:				
	Overall Thoughts:				

Sunday	Date:			Burns Target:	
Notes:	Route:				
	Distance:		Time:		
	Weight:		Speed:		
	Burn Cals:		Heart Rate:		
	Weather:		Breathing:		
	How I Felt:				
	Injuries:				
	Overall Thoughts:				

Weekly Review			
Total Distance:		Weight loss:	
Average Speed:		Total Hours:	
Average Heart Rate:		Total Burns:	
Notes / Thoughts:			

Year: _____ Month: _____ Week: _____ Weekly Goal: _____

Monday	Date:	Burns Target:	
Notes:	Route:		
	Distance:	Time:	
	Weight:	Speed:	
	Burn Cals:	Heart Rate:	
	Weather:	Breathing:	
	How I Felt:		
	Injuries:		
	Overall Thoughts:		

Tuesday	Date:	Burns Target:	
Notes:	Route:		
	Distance:	Time:	
	Weight:	Speed:	
	Burn Cals:	Heart Rate:	
	Weather:	Breathing:	
	How I Felt:		
	Injuries:		
	Overall Thoughts:		

Wednesday	Date:	Burns Target:	
Notes:	Route:		
	Distance:	Time:	
	Weight:	Speed:	
	Burn Cals:	Heart Rate:	
	Weather:	Breathing:	
	How I Felt:		
	Injuries:		
	Overall Thoughts:		

Thursday	Date:	Burns Target:	
Notes:	Route:		
	Distance:	Time:	
	Weight:	Speed:	
	Burn Cals:	Heart Rate:	
	Weather:	Breathing:	
	How I Felt:		
	Injuries:		
	Overall Thoughts:		

Friday	Date:		Burns Target:	
Notes:	Route:			
	Distance:		Time:	
	Weight:		Speed:	
	Burn Cals:		Heart Rate:	
	Weather:		Breathing:	
	How I Felt:			
	Injuries:			
	Overall Thoughts:			

Saturday	Date:		Burns Target:	
Notes:	Route:			
	Distance:		Time:	
	Weight:		Speed:	
	Burn Cals:		Heart Rate:	
	Weather:		Breathing:	
	How I Felt:			
	Injuries:			
	Overall Thoughts:			

Sunday	Date:		Burns Target:	
Notes:	Route:			
	Distance:		Time:	
	Weight:		Speed:	
	Burn Cals:		Heart Rate:	
	Weather:		Breathing:	
	How I Felt:			
	Injuries:			
	Overall Thoughts:			

Weekly Review			
Total Distance:		Weight loss:	
Average Speed:		Total Hours:	
Average Heart Rate:		Total Burns:	
Notes / Thoughts:			

Year: .... Month: .... Week: .... Weekly Goal: ....

Monday	Date:	Burns Target:
Notes:	Route:	
	Distance:	Time:
	Weight:	Speed:
	Burn Cals:	Heart Rate:
	Weather:	Breathing:
	How I Felt:	
	Injuries:	
	Overall Thoughts:	

Tuesday	Date:	Burns Target:
Notes:	Route:	
	Distance:	Time:
	Weight:	Speed:
	Burn Cals:	Heart Rate:
	Weather:	Breathing:
	How I Felt:	
	Injuries:	
	Overall Thoughts:	

Wednesday	Date:	Burns Target:
Notes:	Route:	
	Distance:	Time:
	Weight:	Speed:
	Burn Cals:	Heart Rate:
	Weather:	Breathing:
	How I Felt:	
	Injuries:	
	Overall Thoughts:	

Thursday	Date:	Burns Target:
Notes:	Route:	
	Distance:	Time:
	Weight:	Speed:
	Burn Cals:	Heart Rate:
	Weather:	Breathing:
	How I Felt:	
	Injuries:	
	Overall Thoughts:	

Friday	**Date:**		**Burns Target:**
Notes:	Route:		
	Distance:	Time:	
	Weight:	Speed:	
	Burn Cals:	Heart Rate:	
	Weather:	Breathing:	
	How I Felt:		
	Injuries:		
	Overall Thoughts:		

Saturday	**Date:**		**Burns Target:**
Notes:	Route:		
	Distance:	Time:	
	Weight:	Speed:	
	Burn Cals:	Heart Rate:	
	Weather:	Breathing:	
	How I Felt:		
	Injuries:		
	Overall Thoughts:		

Sunday	**Date:**		**Burns Target:**
Notes:	Route:		
	Distance:	Time:	
	Weight:	Speed:	
	Burn Cals:	Heart Rate:	
	Weather:	Breathing:	
	How I Felt:		
	Injuries:		
	Overall Thoughts:		

Weekly Review			
Total Distance:		Weight loss:	
Average Speed:		Total Hours:	
Average Heart Rate:		Total Burns:	
Notes / Thoughts:			

Year:_____ Month:_____ Week:_____ Weekly Goal:_____

Monday	Date:	Burns Target:
Notes:	Route:	
	Distance:	Time:
	Weight:	Speed:
	Burn Cals:	Heart Rate:
	Weather:	Breathing:
	How I Felt:	
	Injuries:	
	Overall Thoughts:	

Tuesday	Date:	Burns Target:
Notes:	Route:	
	Distance:	Time:
	Weight:	Speed:
	Burn Cals:	Heart Rate:
	Weather:	Breathing:
	How I Felt:	
	Injuries:	
	Overall Thoughts:	

Wednesday	Date:	Burns Target:
Notes:	Route:	
	Distance:	Time:
	Weight:	Speed:
	Burn Cals:	Heart Rate:
	Weather:	Breathing:
	How I Felt:	
	Injuries:	
	Overall Thoughts:	

Thursday	Date:	Burns Target:
Notes:	Route:	
	Distance:	Time:
	Weight:	Speed:
	Burn Cals:	Heart Rate:
	Weather:	Breathing:
	How I Felt:	
	Injuries:	
	Overall Thoughts:	

Friday	Date:		Burns Target:	
Notes:	Route:			
	Distance:		Time:	
	Weight:		Speed:	
	Burn Cals:		Heart Rate:	
	Weather:		Breathing:	
	How I Felt:			
	Injuries:			
	Overall Thoughts:			

Saturday	Date:		Burns Target:	
Notes:	Route:			
	Distance:		Time:	
	Weight:		Speed:	
	Burn Cals:		Heart Rate:	
	Weather:		Breathing:	
	How I Felt:			
	Injuries:			
	Overall Thoughts:			

Sunday	Date:		Burns Target:	
Notes:	Route:			
	Distance:		Time:	
	Weight:		Speed:	
	Burn Cals:		Heart Rate:	
	Weather:		Breathing:	
	How I Felt:			
	Injuries:			
	Overall Thoughts:			

Weekly Review			
Total Distance:		Weight loss:	
Average Speed:		Total Hours:	
Average Heart Rate:		Total Burns:	
Notes / Thoughts:			

Year:_____ Month:_____ Week:_____ Weekly Goal:_____

Monday	Date:	Burns Target:	
Notes:	Route:		
	Distance:	Time:	
	Weight:	Speed:	
	Burn Cals:	Heart Rate:	
	Weather:	Breathing:	
	How I Felt:		
	Injuries:		
	Overall Thoughts:		

Tuesday	Date:	Burns Target:	
Notes:	Route:		
	Distance:	Time:	
	Weight:	Speed:	
	Burn Cals:	Heart Rate:	
	Weather:	Breathing:	
	How I Felt:		
	Injuries:		
	Overall Thoughts:		

Wednesday	Date:	Burns Target:	
Notes:	Route:		
	Distance:	Time:	
	Weight:	Speed:	
	Burn Cals:	Heart Rate:	
	Weather:	Breathing:	
	How I Felt:		
	Injuries:		
	Overall Thoughts:		

Thursday	Date:	Burns Target:	
Notes:	Route:		
	Distance:	Time:	
	Weight:	Speed:	
	Burn Cals:	Heart Rate:	
	Weather:	Breathing:	
	How I Felt:		
	Injuries:		
	Overall Thoughts:		

Friday	Date:	Burns Target:
Notes:	Route:	
	Distance:	Time:
	Weight:	Speed:
	Burn Cals:	Heart Rate:
	Weather:	Breathing:
	How I Felt:	
	Injuries:	
	Overall Thoughts:	

Saturday	Date:	Burns Target:
Notes:	Route:	
	Distance:	Time:
	Weight:	Speed:
	Burn Cals:	Heart Rate:
	Weather:	Breathing:
	How I Felt:	
	Injuries:	
	Overall Thoughts:	

Sunday	Date:	Burns Target:
Notes:	Route:	
	Distance:	Time:
	Weight:	Speed:
	Burn Cals:	Heart Rate:
	Weather:	Breathing:
	How I Felt:	
	Injuries:	
	Overall Thoughts:	

Weekly Review

Total Distance:		Weight loss:	
Average Speed:		Total Hours:	
Average Heart Rate:		Total Burns:	

Notes / Thoughts:

Year:_____ Month:_____ Week:_____ Weekly Goal:_____

Monday	Date:	Burns Target:		
Notes:	Route:			
	Distance:		Time:	
	Weight:		Speed:	
	Burn Cals:		Heart Rate:	
	Weather:		Breathing:	
	How I Felt:			
	Injuries:			
	Overall Thoughts:			

Tuesday	Date:	Burns Target:		
Notes:	Route:			
	Distance:		Time:	
	Weight:		Speed:	
	Burn Cals:		Heart Rate:	
	Weather:		Breathing:	
	How I Felt:			
	Injuries:			
	Overall Thoughts:			

Wednesday	Date:	Burns Target:		
Notes:	Route:			
	Distance:		Time:	
	Weight:		Speed:	
	Burn Cals:		Heart Rate:	
	Weather:		Breathing:	
	How I Felt:			
	Injuries:			
	Overall Thoughts:			

Thursday	Date:	Burns Target:		
Notes:	Route:			
	Distance:		Time:	
	Weight:		Speed:	
	Burn Cals:		Heart Rate:	
	Weather:		Breathing:	
	How I Felt:			
	Injuries:			
	Overall Thoughts:			

Friday	Date:		Burns Target:
Notes:	Route:		
	Distance:	Time:	
	Weight:	Speed:	
	Burn Cals:	Heart Rate:	
	Weather:	Breathing:	
	How I Felt:		
	Injuries:		
	Overall Thoughts:		

Saturday	Date:		Burns Target:
Notes:	Route:		
	Distance:	Time:	
	Weight:	Speed:	
	Burn Cals:	Heart Rate:	
	Weather:	Breathing:	
	How I Felt:		
	Injuries:		
	Overall Thoughts:		

Sunday	Date:		Burns Target:
Notes:	Route:		
	Distance:	Time:	
	Weight:	Speed:	
	Burn Cals:	Heart Rate:	
	Weather:	Breathing:	
	How I Felt:		
	Injuries:		
	Overall Thoughts:		

Weekly Review			
Total Distance:		Weight loss:	
Average Speed:		Total Hours:	
Average Heart Rate:		Total Burns:	
Notes / Thoughts:			

Year:_____ Month:_____ Week:_____ Weekly Goal:_____

Monday	Date:	Burns Target:
Notes:	Route:	
	Distance:	Time:
	Weight:	Speed:
	Burn Cals:	Heart Rate:
	Weather:	Breathing:
	How I Felt:	
	Injuries:	
	Overall Thoughts:	

Tuesday	Date:	Burns Target:
Notes:	Route:	
	Distance:	Time:
	Weight:	Speed:
	Burn Cals:	Heart Rate:
	Weather:	Breathing:
	How I Felt:	
	Injuries:	
	Overall Thoughts:	

Wednesday	Date:	Burns Target:
Notes:	Route:	
	Distance:	Time:
	Weight:	Speed:
	Burn Cals:	Heart Rate:
	Weather:	Breathing:
	How I Felt:	
	Injuries:	
	Overall Thoughts:	

Thursday	Date:	Burns Target:
Notes:	Route:	
	Distance:	Time:
	Weight:	Speed:
	Burn Cals:	Heart Rate:
	Weather:	Breathing:
	How I Felt:	
	Injuries:	
	Overall Thoughts:	

Friday

Date:		Burns Target:

Notes:

Route:	
Distance:	Time:
Weight:	Speed:
Burn Cals:	Heart Rate:
Weather:	Breathing:
How I Felt:	
Injuries:	
Overall Thoughts:	

Saturday

Date:		Burns Target:

Notes:

Route:	
Distance:	Time:
Weight:	Speed:
Burn Cals:	Heart Rate:
Weather:	Breathing:
How I Felt:	
Injuries:	
Overall Thoughts:	

Sunday

Date:		Burns Target:

Notes:

Route:	
Distance:	Time:
Weight:	Speed:
Burn Cals:	Heart Rate:
Weather:	Breathing:
How I Felt:	
Injuries:	
Overall Thoughts:	

Weekly Review

Total Distance:		Weight loss:	
Average Speed:		Total Hours:	
Average Heart Rate:		Total Burns:	

Notes / Thoughts:

Year: .... Month: .... Week: .... Weekly Goal: ....

Monday	Date:		Burns Target:	
Notes:	Route:			
	Distance:		Time:	
	Weight:		Speed:	
	Burn Cals:		Heart Rate:	
	Weather:		Breathing:	
	How I Felt:			
	Injuries:			
	Overall Thoughts:			

Tuesday	Date:		Burns Target:	
Notes:	Route:			
	Distance:		Time:	
	Weight:		Speed:	
	Burn Cals:		Heart Rate:	
	Weather:		Breathing:	
	How I Felt:			
	Injuries:			
	Overall Thoughts:			

Wednesday	Date:		Burns Target:	
Notes:	Route:			
	Distance:		Time:	
	Weight:		Speed:	
	Burn Cals:		Heart Rate:	
	Weather:		Breathing:	
	How I Felt:			
	Injuries:			
	Overall Thoughts:			

Thursday	Date:		Burns Target:	
Notes:	Route:			
	Distance:		Time:	
	Weight:		Speed:	
	Burn Cals:		Heart Rate:	
	Weather:		Breathing:	
	How I Felt:			
	Injuries:			
	Overall Thoughts:			

Friday	Date:		Burns Target:
Notes:	Route:		
	Distance:		Time:
	Weight:		Speed:
	Burn Cals:		Heart Rate:
	Weather:		Breathing:
	How I Felt:		
	Injuries:		
	Overall Thoughts:		

Saturday	Date:		Burns Target:
Notes:	Route:		
	Distance:		Time:
	Weight:		Speed:
	Burn Cals:		Heart Rate:
	Weather:		Breathing:
	How I Felt:		
	Injuries:		
	Overall Thoughts:		

Sunday	Date:		Burns Target:
Notes:	Route:		
	Distance:		Time:
	Weight:		Speed:
	Burn Cals:		Heart Rate:
	Weather:		Breathing:
	How I Felt:		
	Injuries:		
	Overall Thoughts:		

Weekly Review

Total Distance:		Weight loss:	
Average Speed:		Total Hours:	
Average Heart Rate:		Total Burns:	

Notes / Thoughts:

Year: .... Month: .... Week: .... Weekly Goal: ....

Monday	Date:		Burns Target:
Notes:	Route:		
	Distance:		Time:
	Weight:		Speed:
	Burn Cals:		Heart Rate:
	Weather:		Breathing:
	How I Felt:		
	Injuries:		
	Overall Thoughts:		

Tuesday	Date:		Burns Target:
Notes:	Route:		
	Distance:		Time:
	Weight:		Speed:
	Burn Cals:		Heart Rate:
	Weather:		Breathing:
	How I Felt:		
	Injuries:		
	Overall Thoughts:		

Wednesday	Date:		Burns Target:
Notes:	Route:		
	Distance:		Time:
	Weight:		Speed:
	Burn Cals:		Heart Rate:
	Weather:		Breathing:
	How I Felt:		
	Injuries:		
	Overall Thoughts:		

Thursday	Date:		Burns Target:
Notes:	Route:		
	Distance:		Time:
	Weight:		Speed:
	Burn Cals:		Heart Rate:
	Weather:		Breathing:
	How I Felt:		
	Injuries:		
	Overall Thoughts:		

Friday	Date:	Burns Target:
Notes:	Route:	
	Distance:	Time:
	Weight:	Speed:
	Burn Cals:	Heart Rate:
	Weather:	Breathing:
	How I Felt:	
	Injuries:	
	Overall Thoughts:	

Saturday	Date:	Burns Target:
Notes:	Route:	
	Distance:	Time:
	Weight:	Speed:
	Burn Cals:	Heart Rate:
	Weather:	Breathing:
	How I Felt:	
	Injuries:	
	Overall Thoughts:	

Sunday	Date:	Burns Target:
Notes:	Route:	
	Distance:	Time:
	Weight:	Speed:
	Burn Cals:	Heart Rate:
	Weather:	Breathing:
	How I Felt:	
	Injuries:	
	Overall Thoughts:	

Weekly Review

Total Distance:		Weight loss:	
Average Speed:		Total Hours:	
Average Heart Rate:		Total Burns:	

Notes / Thoughts:

Year:_____ Month:_____ Week:_____ Weekly Goal:_____

Monday	Date:	Burns Target:
Notes:	Route:	
	Distance:	Time:
	Weight:	Speed:
	Burn Cals:	Heart Rate:
	Weather:	Breathing:
	How I Felt:	
	Injuries:	
	Overall Thoughts:	

Tuesday	Date:	Burns Target:
Notes:	Route:	
	Distance:	Time:
	Weight:	Speed:
	Burn Cals:	Heart Rate:
	Weather:	Breathing:
	How I Felt:	
	Injuries:	
	Overall Thoughts:	

Wednesday	Date:	Burns Target:
Notes:	Route:	
	Distance:	Time:
	Weight:	Speed:
	Burn Cals:	Heart Rate:
	Weather:	Breathing:
	How I Felt:	
	Injuries:	
	Overall Thoughts:	

Thursday	Date:	Burns Target:
Notes:	Route:	
	Distance:	Time:
	Weight:	Speed:
	Burn Cals:	Heart Rate:
	Weather:	Breathing:
	How I Felt:	
	Injuries:	
	Overall Thoughts:	

Friday	Date:		Burns Target:	
Notes:	Route:			
	Distance:		Time:	
	Weight:		Speed:	
	Burn Cals:		Heart Rate:	
	Weather:		Breathing:	
	How I Felt:			
	Injuries:			
	Overall Thoughts:			

Saturday	Date:		Burns Target:	
Notes:	Route:			
	Distance:		Time:	
	Weight:		Speed:	
	Burn Cals:		Heart Rate:	
	Weather:		Breathing:	
	How I Felt:			
	Injuries:			
	Overall Thoughts:			

Sunday	Date:		Burns Target:	
Notes:	Route:			
	Distance:		Time:	
	Weight:		Speed:	
	Burn Cals:		Heart Rate:	
	Weather:		Breathing:	
	How I Felt:			
	Injuries:			
	Overall Thoughts:			

Weekly Review			
Total Distance:		Weight loss:	
Average Speed:		Total Hours:	
Average Heart Rate:		Total Burns:	
Notes / Thoughts:			

Year:_____ Month:_____ Week:_____ Weekly Goal:_____

Monday	Date:		Burns Target:
Notes:	Route:		
	Distance:	Time:	
	Weight:	Speed:	
	Burn Cals:	Heart Rate:	
	Weather:	Breathing:	
	How I Felt:		
	Injuries:		
	Overall Thoughts:		

Tuesday	Date:		Burns Target:
Notes:	Route:		
	Distance:	Time:	
	Weight:	Speed:	
	Burn Cals:	Heart Rate:	
	Weather:	Breathing:	
	How I Felt:		
	Injuries:		
	Overall Thoughts:		

Wednesday	Date:		Burns Target:
Notes:	Route:		
	Distance:	Time:	
	Weight:	Speed:	
	Burn Cals:	Heart Rate:	
	Weather:	Breathing:	
	How I Felt:		
	Injuries:		
	Overall Thoughts:		

Thursday	Date:		Burns Target:
Notes:	Route:		
	Distance:	Time:	
	Weight:	Speed:	
	Burn Cals:	Heart Rate:	
	Weather:	Breathing:	
	How I Felt:		
	Injuries:		
	Overall Thoughts:		

Friday

Date:		Burns Target:	
Route:			
Distance:		Time:	
Weight:		Speed:	
Burn Cals:		Heart Rate:	
Weather:		Breathing:	
How I Felt:			
Injuries:			
Overall Thoughts:			

Notes:

Saturday

Date:		Burns Target:	
Route:			
Distance:		Time:	
Weight:		Speed:	
Burn Cals:		Heart Rate:	
Weather:		Breathing:	
How I Felt:			
Injuries:			
Overall Thoughts:			

Notes:

Sunday

Date:		Burns Target:	
Route:			
Distance:		Time:	
Weight:		Speed:	
Burn Cals:		Heart Rate:	
Weather:		Breathing:	
How I Felt:			
Injuries:			
Overall Thoughts:			

Notes:

Weekly Review

Total Distance:		Weight loss:	
Average Speed:		Total Hours:	
Average Heart Rate:		Total Burns:	

Notes / Thoughts:

Year: _____ Month: _____ Week: _____ Weekly Goal: _____

Monday	Date:	Burns Target:
Notes:	Route:	
	Distance:	Time:
	Weight:	Speed:
	Burn Cals:	Heart Rate:
	Weather:	Breathing:
	How I Felt:	
	Injuries:	
	Overall Thoughts:	

Tuesday	Date:	Burns Target:
Notes:	Route:	
	Distance:	Time:
	Weight:	Speed:
	Burn Cals:	Heart Rate:
	Weather:	Breathing:
	How I Felt:	
	Injuries:	
	Overall Thoughts:	

Wednesday	Date:	Burns Target:
Notes:	Route:	
	Distance:	Time:
	Weight:	Speed:
	Burn Cals:	Heart Rate:
	Weather:	Breathing:
	How I Felt:	
	Injuries:	
	Overall Thoughts:	

Thursday	Date:	Burns Target:
Notes:	Route:	
	Distance:	Time:
	Weight:	Speed:
	Burn Cals:	Heart Rate:
	Weather:	Breathing:
	How I Felt:	
	Injuries:	
	Overall Thoughts:	

Friday	Date:		Burns Target:
Notes:	Route:		
	Distance:	Time:	
	Weight:	Speed:	
	Burn Cals:	Heart Rate:	
	Weather:	Breathing:	
	How I Felt:		
	Injuries:		
	Overall Thoughts:		

Saturday	Date:		Burns Target:
Notes:	Route:		
	Distance:	Time:	
	Weight:	Speed:	
	Burn Cals:	Heart Rate:	
	Weather:	Breathing:	
	How I Felt:		
	Injuries:		
	Overall Thoughts:		

Sunday	Date:		Burns Target:
Notes:	Route:		
	Distance:	Time:	
	Weight:	Speed:	
	Burn Cals:	Heart Rate:	
	Weather:	Breathing:	
	How I Felt:		
	Injuries:		
	Overall Thoughts:		

Weekly Review			
Total Distance:		Weight loss:	
Average Speed:		Total Hours:	
Average Heart Rate:		Total Burns:	
Notes / Thoughts:			

Year:_____ Month:_____ Week:_____ Weekly Goal:_____

Monday	Date:		Burns Target:	
Notes:	Route:			
	Distance:		Time:	
	Weight:		Speed:	
	Burn Cals:		Heart Rate:	
	Weather:		Breathing:	
	How I Felt:			
	Injuries:			
	Overall Thoughts:			

Tuesday	Date:		Burns Target:	
Notes:	Route:			
	Distance:		Time:	
	Weight:		Speed:	
	Burn Cals:		Heart Rate:	
	Weather:		Breathing:	
	How I Felt:			
	Injuries:			
	Overall Thoughts:			

Wednesday	Date:		Burns Target:	
Notes:	Route:			
	Distance:		Time:	
	Weight:		Speed:	
	Burn Cals:		Heart Rate:	
	Weather:		Breathing:	
	How I Felt:			
	Injuries:			
	Overall Thoughts:			

Thursday	Date:		Burns Target:	
Notes:	Route:			
	Distance:		Time:	
	Weight:		Speed:	
	Burn Cals:		Heart Rate:	
	Weather:		Breathing:	
	How I Felt:			
	Injuries:			
	Overall Thoughts:			

Friday	Date:		Burns Target:	
Notes:	Route:			
	Distance:		Time:	
	Weight:		Speed:	
	Burn Cals:		Heart Rate:	
	Weather:		Breathing:	
	How I Felt:			
	Injuries:			
	Overall Thoughts:			

Saturday	Date:		Burns Target:	
Notes:	Route:			
	Distance:		Time:	
	Weight:		Speed:	
	Burn Cals:		Heart Rate:	
	Weather:		Breathing:	
	How I Felt:			
	Injuries:			
	Overall Thoughts:			

Sunday	Date:		Burns Target:	
Notes:	Route:			
	Distance:		Time:	
	Weight:		Speed:	
	Burn Cals:		Heart Rate:	
	Weather:		Breathing:	
	How I Felt:			
	Injuries:			
	Overall Thoughts:			

Weekly Review

Total Distance:		Weight loss:	
Average Speed:		Total Hours:	
Average Heart Rate:		Total Burns:	

Notes / Thoughts:

Year:_____ Month:_____ Week:_____ Weekly Goal:_____

Monday	Date:		Burns Target:	
Notes:	Route:			
	Distance:		Time:	
	Weight:		Speed:	
	Burn Cals:		Heart Rate:	
	Weather:		Breathing:	
	How I Felt:			
	Injuries:			
	Overall Thoughts:			

Tuesday	Date:		Burns Target:	
Notes:	Route:			
	Distance:		Time:	
	Weight:		Speed:	
	Burn Cals:		Heart Rate:	
	Weather:		Breathing:	
	How I Felt:			
	Injuries:			
	Overall Thoughts:			

Wednesday	Date:		Burns Target:	
Notes:	Route:			
	Distance:		Time:	
	Weight:		Speed:	
	Burn Cals:		Heart Rate:	
	Weather:		Breathing:	
	How I Felt:			
	Injuries:			
	Overall Thoughts:			

Thursday	Date:		Burns Target:	
Notes:	Route:			
	Distance:		Time:	
	Weight:		Speed:	
	Burn Cals:		Heart Rate:	
	Weather:		Breathing:	
	How I Felt:			
	Injuries:			
	Overall Thoughts:			

Friday	Date:		Burns Target:
Notes:	Route:		
	Distance:		Time:
	Weight:		Speed:
	Burn Cals:		Heart Rate:
	Weather:		Breathing:
	How I Felt:		
	Injuries:		
	Overall Thoughts:		

Saturday	Date:		Burns Target:
Notes:	Route:		
	Distance:		Time:
	Weight:		Speed:
	Burn Cals:		Heart Rate:
	Weather:		Breathing:
	How I Felt:		
	Injuries:		
	Overall Thoughts:		

Sunday	Date:		Burns Target:
Notes:	Route:		
	Distance:		Time:
	Weight:		Speed:
	Burn Cals:		Heart Rate:
	Weather:		Breathing:
	How I Felt:		
	Injuries:		
	Overall Thoughts:		

Weekly Review

Total Distance:		Weight loss:	
Average Speed:		Total Hours:	
Average Heart Rate:		Total Burns:	

Notes / Thoughts:

Year: _____ Month: _____ Week: _____ Weekly Goal: _____

Monday	Date:	Burns Target:
Notes:	Route:	
	Distance:	Time:
	Weight:	Speed:
	Burn Cals:	Heart Rate:
	Weather:	Breathing:
	How I Felt:	
	Injuries:	
	Overall Thoughts:	

Tuesday	Date:	Burns Target:
Notes:	Route:	
	Distance:	Time:
	Weight:	Speed:
	Burn Cals:	Heart Rate:
	Weather:	Breathing:
	How I Felt:	
	Injuries:	
	Overall Thoughts:	

Wednesday	Date:	Burns Target:
Notes:	Route:	
	Distance:	Time:
	Weight:	Speed:
	Burn Cals:	Heart Rate:
	Weather:	Breathing:
	How I Felt:	
	Injuries:	
	Overall Thoughts:	

Thursday	Date:	Burns Target:
Notes:	Route:	
	Distance:	Time:
	Weight:	Speed:
	Burn Cals:	Heart Rate:
	Weather:	Breathing:
	How I Felt:	
	Injuries:	
	Overall Thoughts:	

Friday	Date:	Burns Target:	
Notes:	Route:		
	Distance:	Time:	
	Weight:	Speed:	
	Burn Cals:	Heart Rate:	
	Weather:	Breathing:	
	How I Felt:		
	Injuries:		
	Overall Thoughts:		

Saturday	Date:	Burns Target:	
Notes:	Route:		
	Distance:	Time:	
	Weight:	Speed:	
	Burn Cals:	Heart Rate:	
	Weather:	Breathing:	
	How I Felt:		
	Injuries:		
	Overall Thoughts:		

Sunday	Date:	Burns Target:	
Notes:	Route:		
	Distance:	Time:	
	Weight:	Speed:	
	Burn Cals:	Heart Rate:	
	Weather:	Breathing:	
	How I Felt:		
	Injuries:		
	Overall Thoughts:		

Weekly Review

Total Distance:		Weight loss:	
Average Speed:		Total Hours:	
Average Heart Rate:		Total Burns:	

Notes / Thoughts:

Year: .... Month: .... Week: .... Weekly Goal: ....

Monday	Date:		Burns Target:
Notes:	Route:		
	Distance:	Time:	
	Weight:	Speed:	
	Burn Cals:	Heart Rate:	
	Weather:	Breathing:	
	How I Felt:		
	Injuries:		
	Overall Thoughts:		

Tuesday	Date:		Burns Target:
Notes:	Route:		
	Distance:	Time:	
	Weight:	Speed:	
	Burn Cals:	Heart Rate:	
	Weather:	Breathing:	
	How I Felt:		
	Injuries:		
	Overall Thoughts:		

Wednesday	Date:		Burns Target:
Notes:	Route:		
	Distance:	Time:	
	Weight:	Speed:	
	Burn Cals:	Heart Rate:	
	Weather:	Breathing:	
	How I Felt:		
	Injuries:		
	Overall Thoughts:		

Thursday	Date:		Burns Target:
Notes:	Route:		
	Distance:	Time:	
	Weight:	Speed:	
	Burn Cals:	Heart Rate:	
	Weather:	Breathing:	
	How I Felt:		
	Injuries:		
	Overall Thoughts:		

Friday	Date:		Burns Target:
Notes:	Route:		
	Distance:	Time:	
	Weight:	Speed:	
	Burn Cals:	Heart Rate:	
	Weather:	Breathing:	
	How I Felt:		
	Injuries:		
	Overall Thoughts:		

Saturday	Date:		Burns Target:
Notes:	Route:		
	Distance:	Time:	
	Weight:	Speed:	
	Burn Cals:	Heart Rate:	
	Weather:	Breathing:	
	How I Felt:		
	Injuries:		
	Overall Thoughts:		

Sunday	Date:		Burns Target:
Notes:	Route:		
	Distance:	Time:	
	Weight:	Speed:	
	Burn Cals:	Heart Rate:	
	Weather:	Breathing:	
	How I Felt:		
	Injuries:		
	Overall Thoughts:		

Weekly Review			
Total Distance:		Weight loss:	
Average Speed:		Total Hours:	
Average Heart Rate:		Total Burns:	
Notes / Thoughts:			

Year:_____ Month:_____ Week:_____ Weekly Goal:_____

Monday	Date:	Burns Target:
Notes:	Route:	
	Distance:	Time:
	Weight:	Speed:
	Burn Cals:	Heart Rate:
	Weather:	Breathing:
	How I Felt:	
	Injuries:	
	Overall Thoughts:	

Tuesday	Date:	Burns Target:
Notes:	Route:	
	Distance:	Time:
	Weight:	Speed:
	Burn Cals:	Heart Rate:
	Weather:	Breathing:
	How I Felt:	
	Injuries:	
	Overall Thoughts:	

Wednesday	Date:	Burns Target:
Notes:	Route:	
	Distance:	Time:
	Weight:	Speed:
	Burn Cals:	Heart Rate:
	Weather:	Breathing:
	How I Felt:	
	Injuries:	
	Overall Thoughts:	

Thursday	Date:	Burns Target:
Notes:	Route:	
	Distance:	Time:
	Weight:	Speed:
	Burn Cals:	Heart Rate:
	Weather:	Breathing:
	How I Felt:	
	Injuries:	
	Overall Thoughts:	

Friday	Date:		Burns Target:
Notes:	Route:		
	Distance:		Time:
	Weight:		Speed:
	Burn Cals:		Heart Rate:
	Weather:		Breathing:
	How I Felt:		
	Injuries:		
	Overall Thoughts:		

Saturday	Date:		Burns Target:
Notes:	Route:		
	Distance:		Time:
	Weight:		Speed:
	Burn Cals:		Heart Rate:
	Weather:		Breathing:
	How I Felt:		
	Injuries:		
	Overall Thoughts:		

Sunday	Date:		Burns Target:
Notes:	Route:		
	Distance:		Time:
	Weight:		Speed:
	Burn Cals:		Heart Rate:
	Weather:		Breathing:
	How I Felt:		
	Injuries:		
	Overall Thoughts:		

Weekly Review

Total Distance:		Weight loss:	
Average Speed:		Total Hours:	
Average Heart Rate:		Total Burns:	

Notes / Thoughts:

Made in the USA
Columbia, SC
23 August 2019